Windows Troubleshooting Series

Mike Halsey, MVP
Series Editor

Apress®

Windows Installation and Update Troubleshooting

Chris Rhodes, MVP
Andrew Bettany, MVP

Apress®

Windows Installation and Update Troubleshooting

Chris Rhodes
Huddersfield, United Kingdom

Andrew Bettany
York, North Yorkshire, United Kingdom

ISBN-13 (pbk): 978-1-4842-1826-6
DOI 10.1007/978-1-4842-1827-3

ISBN-13 (electronic): 978-1-4842-1827-3

Library of Congress Control Number: 2016955433

Managing Director: Welmoed Spahr
Lead Editor: Gwenan Spearing
Technical Reviewers: Dustin Harper and Zeshan Sattar
Editorial Board: Steve Anglin, Pramila Balan, Laura Berendson, Aaron Black,
    Louise Corrigan, Jonathan Gennick, Robert Hutchinson, Celestin Suresh John,
    Nikhil Karkal, James Markham, Susan McDermott, Matthew Moodie, Natalie Pao,
    Gwenan Spearing
Coordinating Editor: Mark Powers
Copy Editor: April Rondeau
Compositor: SPi Global
Indexer: SPi Global
Artist: SPi Global

Distributed to the book trade worldwide by Springer Science+Business Media New York, 233 Spring Street, 6th Floor, New York, NY 10013. Phone 1-800-SPRINGER, fax (201) 348-4505, e-mail orders-ny@springer-sbm.com, or visit www.springeronline.com. Apress Media, LLC is a California LLC and the sole member (owner) is Springer Science + Business Media Finance Inc (SSBM Finance Inc). SSBM Finance Inc is a **Delaware** corporation.

For information on translations, please e-mail rights@apress.com, or visit www.apress.com.

Apress and friends of ED books may be purchased in bulk for academic, corporate, or promotional use. eBook versions and licenses are also available for most titles. For more information, reference our Special Bulk Sales–eBook Licensing web page at www.apress.com/bulk-sales.

Any source code or other supplementary materials referenced by the author in this text are available to readers at www.apress.com/9781484218266. For detailed information about how to locate your book's source code, go to www.apress.com/source-code/. Readers can also access source code at SpringerLink in the Supplementary Material section for each chapter.

Printed on acid-free paper

Contents at a Glance

Contents

About the Authors

Chris Rhodes is a Microsoft MVP (Most Valuable Professional) awardee and technical expert. Over nearly two decades as a Microsoft Certified Trainer, he has taught Windows technologies to thousands of students, taking them to certification level and beyond. Outside of the classroom, Chris has been involved with numerous projects, including consulting for a variety of customers, and also as a subject matter expert for Microsoft on several projects. In his spare time, Chris can often be found attending and speaking at conferences, such as TechEd and MCT and MVP events. Chris is also a founding member of the Windows User Group in the United Kingdom, where he regularly presents with a passion on topics around Windows.

Andrew Bettany is a Microsoft Most Valuable Professional (MVP), recognized for his Windows expertise, and author of several publications including Windows exam certification prep and Microsoft official training materials.

Managed the IT Academy at the University of York, UK for 8 years, and now focuses his time training and writing. As a Microsoft Certified Trainer, Andrew delivers learning and consultancy to businesses on a number of technical areas including Windows deployment and troubleshooting.

He has created and manages the IT Masterclasses series of short intensive technical courses, found at www.itmasterclasses.com and run through his own training company, Deliver IT Training Ltd.

Passionate about learning and helping others, he frequently donates his time to work with Microsoft. He is a frequent speaker and proctor at TechEd conferences worldwide. In 2011 he delivered a "train the trainer" class in earthquake-hit Haiti to help the community rebuild their technology skills, and he returned in November 2013 to deliver a second bootcamp.

Andrew is very active on social media and can be found on LinkedIn, Facebook, and Twitter. He lives in a village just outside of the beautiful city of York in Yorkshire, UK.

About the Technical Reviewers

Dustin Harper is an IT professional for a large winery in the United States. He volunteers his time and knowledge among various Microsoft technologies, both in person and online. He was first awarded the Microsoft Most Valuable Professional (MVP) award in 2014. He is active on his website (MSTechpages.com), Microsoft Answers, and other tech forums. He also has several industry certifications, including Microsoft Certified Professional (MCP).

Zeshan Sattar is Head of Curriculum Development at Agilisys Arch, an Apprenticeships Training Provider in the United Kingdom. He is responsible for devising the training and certification curriculum for apprentices between 16 and 24 years old. This includes a diverse range of topics across the infrastructure and development tracks. He has delivered training to audiences across the world, both in person and via online platforms. Zeshan has also worked and spoken at a number of Microsoft events, including Microsoft Ignite and TechEd.

Windows Troubleshooting Series

When something goes wrong with technology, it can seem impossible to diagnose and repair the problem, and harder still to prevent a recurrence. In this series of books, we'll take you inside the workings of your devices and software and teach you how to find and fix problems using a simple step-by-step approach that helps you understand the cause, the solution, and the tools required.

Series Editor
Mike Halsey, MVP

Mike Halsey is a Microsoft MVP (Most Valuable Professional) awardee since 2011, the author of more than ten books on Microsoft Windows, and a teacher of many years. He understands the need to convey subjects that can sometimes be complex in clear and non-intimidating ways.

The Windows Troubleshooting Series is, he feels, a great example of how quality help, support, and tutorials can be delivered to individuals of all technical abilities. He hopes you enjoy reading this and many other books in this series, both now and for years to come.

Introduction

Nearly all PCs purchased contain a version of Microsoft Windows that has been pre-installed by the vendor or manufacturer. The vast majority of Windows users will use the original operating system for the lifetime of the device. Microsoft has always allowed you to change and modify the PC configuration, adding or removing components and allowing users to re-install or change the version of Windows to another version that you may have. This flexibility is one of the reasons that the PC and Windows became very popular to business customers and PC enthusiasts.

Virtualization tools such as Hyper-V allow you to test, evaluate, and use multiple instances of the same or different Windows installation on a single device. For machines that do not support virtualization, or when a user wants the option to choose the version of Windows they want to use as the host, a user can also create multi-boot scenarios where the device has multiple operating systems installed and the user is required to choose the host operating system at boot time.

With Windows XP no longer being supported by Microsoft (since April 8, 2014), this book will focus on the technologies available for the installation, upgrading, and deployment of Windows post–Windows XP. Some tools and concepts used during installation and upgrading have remained relatively static since Windows Vista, such as the WAIK, Sysprep, and the WIM format, but many have been improved upon and expanded. There are plenty of new tools that have been introduced recently including the Windows Assessment and Deployment Kit (ADK), Windows Imaging and Configuration Designer (Windows ICD), Refresh, and Reset, which offer a variety of options when considering an in-place upgrade or new installation of Windows.

If you are upgrading from one version of Windows to a newer version, or upgrading the edition of the same Windows version, the process has become easier and can be fully automated, with all your files and settings optionally being preserved during the upgrade.

Within corporate environments, you are able to use a variety of deployment tools, such as Windows Pre-installation Environment (Windows PE), Deployment Image Servicing and Management (DISM), Windows System Image Manager (Windows SIM), Microsoft Deployment Toolkit (MDT), Windows Deployment Services (Windows DS), and System Center 2012 Configuration Manager (SCCM). New and updated methodologies, including Refresh, Provisioning, and Migration, allow deployments to be quicker, more efficient, and more cost effective.

The threat of malware attacks continues to increase, aiming to disrupt or exploit security vulnerabilities and access your business or personal data and your bank account. You must ensure that your systems remain fully patched and updated. We will discuss Windows Update and review troubleshooting scenarios where a bad update needs to be blocked. Windows Server Update Services (WSUS) offers enterprises the ability to control and scale the approval of updates, and the new peer sharing of updates within Windows 10 allows updates to be rapidly deployed across the network to clients.

More devices are connected to the Internet than ever before, and working anywhere, using either company-owned devices or BYOD, is increasingly popular. The cloud-based Microsoft Intune dashboard offers IT administrators a desktop and mobile-device management solution that helps organizations manage and maintain devices, both those that are decentralized and those based within the office. Intune is included as part of Microsoft's Enterprise Mobility Suite.

CHAPTER 1

■ ■ ■

An Introduction to Windows Installation Methodologies and Tools

With the release of Windows Vista in January 2007, Microsoft introduced a number of new technologies that can be used for deployment; each subsequent version of Windows has improved many of these tools and introduced some new ones.

If you are familiar with some of the Windows deployment tools, you should review this chapter to look for the improved-upon tools. If your experience relates to the Windows XP era, you will be pleased to learn that the Microsoft tools available have been improved greatly and that many have matured into some excellent utilities for you to use.

Some tools are built into Windows, such as Sysprep and Deployment Image Servicing and Management Technical (DISM), while other deployment tools are available by downloading them from the Microsoft Download Center.

This chapter will introduce the tools and methodologies used to install, upgrade, and deploy Windows that will form the foundation of the more advanced topics, which will be covered in the remaining chapters.

From Floppy Disks to Cloud Installation

The Windows installation process has come a long way in the last 20 years. Windows 98 could be installed one file at a time, copied by the setup program from 38 1.68 MB floppy disks. With Windows XP, a bootable CD-ROM drive was still very rare, and you could obtain or create the Windows XP setup boot disks from Microsoft. The Windows XP setup required six floppy disks just to install the setup program, then provided access to the remaining installation files held on the Windows XP CD-ROM.

With Windows Vista through to Windows 8.1, Microsoft moved to a new image-based installation format that used the Windows Image (WIM) file format. Each WIM contained the entire operating system, which could be mounted, maintained, and updated easily using new the deployment tools.

© Chris Rhodes and Andrew Bettany 2016
C. Rhodes and A. Bettany, *Windows Installation and Update Troubleshooting*,
DOI 10.1007/978-1-4842-1827-3_1

Although Windows 10 retains many of the same WIM components that its predecessors had, Windows 10 offers another change in the way that Windows is updated and maintained. Windows Update now provides the ability to deliver both security and driver updates and also new feature upgrades to Windows 10, while the new provisioning packages feature allows the direct deployment of updates and features to a live system.

Understanding the Windows Boot Process

Before we discuss the various options for installing and deploying Windows, we should first review the new startup process that has replaced the old Ntldr process that existed with Windows XP. Ntldr has been replaced by the Windows Boot Manager and the Windows Boot Loader. The boot.ini file has been replaced by the boot configuration data (BCD) registry file.

The simplified boot process for Windows Vista and later versions of Windows is illustrated in Figure 1-1.

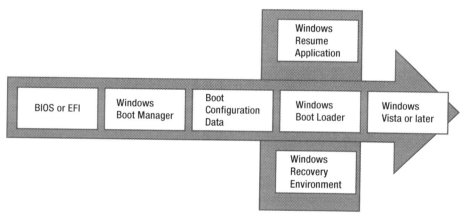

Figure 1-1. Windows boot process

Some of the components of the BCD file are shown in Table 1-1.

Table 1-1. *Boot Components*

File/Process	Description
BCD	Boot Configuration Data (BCD) store, a registry-like database that replaced boot.ini with a more robust and flexible file
WinRE	Replaces the command-line recovery console with a GUI recovery option
Windows Boot Loader	\Windows\System32\WinLoad.exe
Windows Boot Manager	BootMgr is read-only and hidden and is located in the root directory of the active partition
Windows Memory Diagnostic	\Boot\MemTest.exe
Windows Resume Application	Used to restore Windows from hibernation: \Windows\System32\WinResume.exe

The BCD registry file is located in the following location based on the motherboard type:

- BIOS-based systems: \Boot\Bcd on the active partition
- Extensible Firmware Interface (EFI)–based systems: \EFI\ Microsoft\Boot\ folder on the EFI system partition

There are several ways in which you can view and modify the entries in the BCD registry file, as listed in Table 1-2.

Table 1-2. *Methods of Modifying the BCD*

Tool/Utility	Description
Startup and Recovery	Within the Advanced tab of the System Properties dialog box, there are several options for selecting the default operating system to boot up and for configuring the time delay after which the boot menu will appear.
System Configuration Utility (Msconfig.exe)	Troubleshooting GUI tool you can use to configure startup options
BCD Windows Management Instrumentation provider	The Windows Management Instrumentation (WMI) allows you to script utilities that modify the BCD. More information can be found at https://msdn.microsoft.com/library/aa362675.aspx
BCDEdit.exe	BCDEdit.exe is a command-line utility that replaced Bootcfg.exe, which was available in Windows XP. BCDEdit requires an administrative command prompt. You can type bcdedit.exe to view the contents of the BCD registry file, as shown in Figure 1-2.
Third-party tools	There are several third-party tools that allow you to edit the BCD registry file using a GUI, including the following: DualBootPRO (http://www.dualbootpro.org/) EasyBCD (https://neosmart.net/EasyBCD/) Visual BCD Editor (http://www.boyans.net/)

If you open an administrative command prompt and type bcdedit.exe, the contents of your BCD registry file will be displayed, as shown in Figure 1-2.

```
■ Administrator: Command Prompt

Microsoft Windows [Version 10.0.10240]
(c) 2015 Microsoft Corporation. All rights reserved.

C:\WINDOWS\system32>bcdedit

Windows Boot Manager
--------------------
identifier              {bootmgr}
device                  partition=\Device\HarddiskVolume2
path                    \EFI\Microsoft\Boot\bootmgfw.efi
description             Windows Boot Manager
locale                  en-US
inherit                 {globalsettings}
default                 {current}
resumeobject            {c5389709-680a-11e5-9a5d-dd6de921d637}
displayorder            {current}
toolsdisplayorder       {memdiag}
timeout                 30

Windows Boot Loader
-------------------
identifier              {current}
device                  partition=C:
path                    \WINDOWS\system32\winload.efi
description             Windows 10
locale                  en-US
inherit                 {bootloadersettings}
recoverysequence        {c538970b-680a-11e5-9a5d-dd6de921d637}
recoveryenabled         Yes
isolatedcontext         Yes
allowedinmemorysettings 0x15000075
osdevice                partition=C:
systemroot              \WINDOWS
resumeobject            {c5389709-680a-11e5-9a5d-dd6de921d637}
nx                      OptIn
bootmenupolicy          Standard

C:\WINDOWS\system32>_
```

Figure 1-2. Using the BCDedit.exe command to view the BCD contents

BCDedit is a powerful tool, and care should be taken when modifying the file, as your system may not boot if you incorrectly edit the file. For detailed information relating to the BCDedit utility, type bcdedit.exe /?.

To display detailed information about a parameter or switch, type bcdedit.exe /? <Parameter>.

For example, bcdedit.exe /? /createstore.

Understanding the Hardware Abstraction Layer

In older versions of Windows, the hardware abstraction layer (HAL) component, typically the dynamic link library file called Hal.dll, created significant problems when you attempted to move a Windows installation from one system to a newer system; for example, after a system failure. A backup image of Windows XP or Windows Server 2003 was not hardware independent, and any recovered system had to be restored back onto identical hardware.

The purpose of the HAL is to create a separation between the operating system and the physical hardware components on the motherboard. In simple terms, the HAL provides the necessary drivers for communicating with the computer's processor and memory.

Windows Vista and later releases incorporate the ability to automatically detect which HAL should be used at boot time. The detect HAL feature, which is an option that can be set within the BCD, is most often used when the device has multiple operating systems installed, such as in a dual-boot scenario.

For Vista only, there was a setting hidden within the System Configuration Utility (MSConfig.exe) called Detect HAL, which allowed you to force the operating system to search for the different versions of the HAL during deployment. If multiple options were available, Windows would then add a prompt into your boot menu so you could choose which operating system to boot.

■ **Note**   The Detect HAL option within the System Configuration Utility was deprecated in Windows 7 and later. To configure this setting, you would use the BCDEdit tool and use the command bcdedit /set {current} detecthal yes.

Introduction to Windows Deployment Tools

Some of the common tools and features available for Windows installation and deployment are provided freely by Microsoft. However, you need to understand some of the underlying technologies that relate to Windows installation and deployment before we cover the enterprise tools later in this book.

We will cover the following tools in this section:

- Cabinet files

- Windows Imaging Format

- Windows Setup

- Sysprep

- ImageX

- DiskPart

- PowerShell

The Windows Assessment and Deployment Kit (ADK), which replaces the Windows Automated Installation Kit (Windows AIK), is covered later in this chapter.

Cabinet Files

Cabinet (.cab) files are frequently used by older versions of Windows to hold installation files in a compressed status until they are required by the setup program. If a file is too large even when compressed, the .cab file can be spread over several .cab files.

You may still encounter .cab files today, as they are commonly used to reduce file size and download time when obtaining files from the Internet or from a corporate intranet server. Some third-party independent software vendors (ISVs), such as InstallShield and WISE, use the .cab format for installation purposes.

Windows Imaging Format

You should be familiar with the .zip or .rar file extensions–files that contain compressed files. First introduced with Windows Vista, the Windows Imaging format (WIM) is a file-based disk image format that allows Windows to highly compress files relating to the installation of a Windows operating system. In each .wim file you can store multiple operating system images.

Image-based setup is used in high-volume deployment scenarios, such as in an enterprise environment. Images can also be maintained individually or in an ad-hoc manner by using tools such as Deployment Image Servicing and Management (DISM.exe), which can patch or install software updates directly into the WIM file.

The simplified logical layout of a WIM file structure is shown in Figure 1-3.

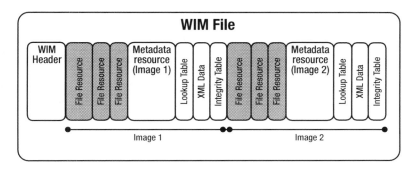

Figure 1-3. *Structure of Windows Imaging file format*

There are six optional components contained within a WIM file, as follows:

- WIM Header – Content definition and resource information, including various .wim file attributes, such as version, size, and compression type

- File Resources – Packages containing data, such as source files

- Metadata Resource – One metadata resource component in each image in a `.wim` file. Contains information relating to how the data is organized in the `.wim` file, such as directory structure and file attributes

- Lookup Table – Information relating to resource file memory locations in the `.wim` file

- XML Data – Contains additional data about the image. To view the XML data, you should use the `Dism /Get-ImageInfo` command.

- Integrity Table – A security hash used to verify the integrity of an image

Windows Setup

The setup executable (now called `Setup.exe`) for Windows installs can be set with various parameters to control how the Windows image (`.wim`) file behaves during the installation. When `Setup.exe` is used with an answer file, the installation process can be fully automated. The `unattend.xml` answer file format replaces the answer files used in earlier versions of Windows, such as `unattend.txt`, `Sysprep.inf`, or `winnt.sif`.

Some common Windows Setup command-line options include the following:

- `Setup /unattend:\\server\share\unattend.xml` (Enables you to use an answer file with Windows Setup)

- `Setup /wds /wdsdiscover /wdsserver:MyWDSServer` (Specifies the name of the Windows Deployment Services server that the client should connect to)

- `Setup /installfrom:D:\custom.wim` (Specifies a different `Install.wim` file to use during Windows Setup)

Windows is installed in stages. The phases of a Windows installation are known as *configuration passes*. Later in this chapter, you will learn that you can create unattended installations using an answer file. The answer file can customize the installation by applying changes in one or more of the configuration passes. The diagram shown in Figure 1-4 shows the configuration passes that are available for the Windows Setup.

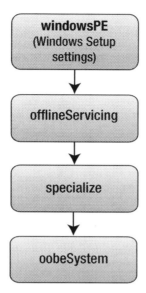

Figure 1-4. *Windows Setup.exe configuration passes*

The four configuration passes that Setup.exe will apply are as follows:

- windowsPE – This is used to specify which Windows image to install and to configure the disk, volumes, and formatting and install boot-critical drivers

- offlineServicing - This configuration pass is used to apply the Windows image to a hard disk and to apply updates, drivers, or language packs.

- specialize - After the Windows image boots for the first time, unique security IDs (SIDs) are created and many Windows features and hardware-specific settings are configured.

- oobeSystem - During this configuration pass, settings are applied to Windows before the Windows Welcome starts, such as to create user accounts, specify language, and set locale settings.

Sysprep

The System Preparation tool (Sysprep) has been available since Windows NT 4.0 and is used for Windows operating system deployment. The version that is included in Windows Vista and later allows you to prepare an operating system for cloning using the WIM disk image format. When combined with an answer file, Sysprep can be used to fully automate the deployment of new computers using the configuration settings contained in the answer file.

Answer files are created using the Windows System Image Manager, which will be discussed later in this chapter.

If you run Sysprep without an answer file, the tool will generalize the Windows installation, which removes all personal settings, user profiles, drivers, hardware profiles, and any saved restore points. When Windows is restarted, Windows Setup will apply the specialize configuration pass only and presents you with the out-of-box experience (OOBE) with the Windows Welcome screen. At this screen you can then customize your system, create user accounts, name the computer, and perform other tasks.

Since Windows 8.1, the Sysprep graphical user interface (GUI) as shown in Figure 1-5 has been deprecated, but it still exists and is supported.

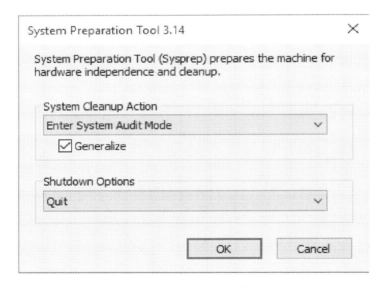

Figure 1-5. *Using the Sysprep tool to generalize Windows*

It is not possible to specify an answer file when using the GUI tool. You should use an elevated command prompt and use the command-line tool sysprep.exe to initiate Sysprep. This file is located in the C:\Windows\System32\Sysprep folder.

There are two main options available to you when using Sysprep, as follows:

1. `Sysprep /audit` – Restarts the computer into audit mode. Audit mode is used to test and evaluate the installation of Windows that is being prepared for deployment. In Audit mode you can continue to add additional drivers or applications to Windows and either use the `Sysprep /audit` setting again or use `Sysprep /generalize`.

2. `Sysprep /generalize` – Prepares the system for imaging and removes unique information from your Windows installation. Sysprep resets the security ID (SID), clears any system restore points, and deletes event logs. Normally it is used with the `/shutdown` switch.

The command-line options available for Sysprep are listed in Table 1-3, and the syntax is as follows:

```
sysprep.exe [/oobe | /audit] [/generalize] [/reboot | /shutdown | /quit]
[/quiet] [/unattend:answerfile]
```

Table 1-3. *Sysprep Command-Line Options*

Option	Description	Example usage
/audit	Restarts the computer into audit mode	Sysprep /audit
/generalize	Prepares the Windows installation to be imaged	Sysprep / generalize / shutdown
/oobe	Restarts the computer into OOBE mode	Sysprep / generalize / shutdown /oobe
/mode:vm	Generalizes a Virtual Hard Disk (VHD). You can only run VM mode from inside a VM.	Sysprep / generalize /oobe /mode:vm
/reboot	Restarts the computer	
/shutdown	Shuts down the computer after the Sysprep command completes	
/quiet	Useful for scripting; Sysprep will run without displaying on-screen confirmation messages	
/quit	Closes the Sysprep tool after the Sysprep command completes	
/unattend:<answerfile>	Applies settings in an answer file to Windows during an unattended installation	Sysprep / audit /reboot / unattend:F:\ Unattend.xml

Sysprep will remove any unique configurations that have been applied to the installation. During the "generalization" process existing elements, including Computer name, Security Identifier (SID), and the Driver Cache will be discarded and will be rebuilt during the reboot sequence.

▒ **More Info**   You can find more information on the Sysprep (System Preparation) Overview Hardware Dev Center page. This page also contains links to resources related to creating the answer files that you use with Sysprep: `https://msdn.microsoft.com/library/windows/hardware/dn938335(v=vs.85).aspx`

ImageX

This command-line tool, introduced in Windows Vista, was one of the first tools that allowed you to capture, modify, and apply WIM images. The version available with Windows 7 allowed you to mount multiple images simultaneously with an increased reliability over that in Windows Vista.

ImageX has been deprecated in Windows 8, and DISM is the replacement tool when managing and servicing images. ImageX is included in this book for reference only; you should use DISM wherever possible.

DiskPart

DiskPart is a command-line utility that allows you to manage Windows disks and volumes. Although many of the tasks are similar to the Disk Management snap-in within Windows, with DiskPart you can perform a superset of the actions that are supported by the GUI.

To launch DiskPart, follow these steps:

1. Open an elevated command prompt, or use Windows+X and choose Command Prompt (Admin).

2. Type `DiskPart` and press Enter.

3. After DiskPart loads, the cursor will show `DISKPART>`.

4. To obtain detailed help with examples of a command, type `HELP` followed by the command. For example, `HELP LIST` provides the syntax that DiskPart uses.

5. To exit DiskPart, type `EXIT` and press Enter, then close the command window.

`DiskPart.exe` offers the ability to script disk management using the command prompt or PowerShell.

▓ **Note**   You can abbreviate most of the DiskPart commands. For example, you can use SEL instead of SELECT or PART instead of PARTITION.

PowerShell

This is the tool of choice for system administrators who manage a large number of client machines or servers. PowerShell offers a fully scriptable and extensible object-oriented programming language that is fully embedded in all modern versions of Windows, including client and server operating systems.

Unlike previous versions of Windows where GUI snap-ins were the predominant admin tools, a great many administrative actions can now only be performed using PowerShell. New services such as Office 365 and Microsoft Azure utilize PowerShell for nearly all administrative tasks.

This book does not have the room to cover PowerShell in much detail, but, where possible, references to PowerShell will be included. If you are unfamiliar with PowerShell, you should review the potential that PowerShell offers, especially if you manage a large number of devices or users.

The Windows Assessment and Deployment Kit

The Windows Assessment and Deployment Kit (ADK) replaces the Windows Automated Installation Kit (Windows AIK) and includes a number of powerful tools and wizards that allow you to fully customize your Windows deployments by creating images and provisioning packages.

The ADK is used for Windows 8 and later, and the AIK was used for Windows Vista and Windows 7 installations. The tools are backward compatible, and therefore you should ensure that you use the latest version of the toolkit.

The latest version of the ADK is compatible with Windows 10 and includes the following key tools, which will be introduced in this chapter:

- Windows System Image Manager
- Windows Preinstallation Environment
- Deployment Image Servicing and Management
- Windows Imaging and Configuration Designer
- Windows Assessment Toolkit
- Windows Performance Toolkit

▓ **More Info**   You can download the Windows ADK from https://msdn.microsoft.com/windows/hardware/dn913721.aspx

---

When you install the ADK you should ensure that the required deployment tools and features are installed. You should review the installation options in each feature, as shown in Figure 1-6.

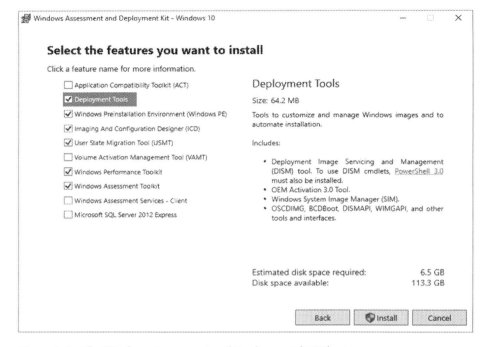

Figure 1-6. *The Windows Assessment and Deployment (ADK) setup*

Windows System Image Manager

First introduced in Windows Vista, the Windows System Image Manager (Windows SIM) is used for creating and editing answer files (Unattend.xml), which can be used to automate the installation of all versions of Windows from Windows Vista and later.

The Windows SIM is included in the Windows Assessment and Deployment Kit (ADK) and is compatible with Windows 8 and later, and is also found in the Windows Automated Installation Toolkit (AIK), which is used with Windows Vista and Windows 7 only. Both toolkits can be used for the following high-level scenarios:

- Create a new answer file to be applied to a Windows image during installation

- Edit an existing answer file

- Add additional device drivers to an answer file

- Add applications or additional drivers to an answer file

- Add updates to a Windows image offline

- Create a configuration set of distribution files

- Import packages to a distribution share available for deployment

Examples of installation tasks that you can configure in an answer file using the Windows SIM include the following:

- Partition and format hard disks

- Install windows

- Add or change language packs and settings

- Modify video display settings

- Create the computer name

- Install third-party applications

- Install device drivers

- Add activation keys for Windows and Office

- Add user accounts

- Add Windows updates and upgrades

When you first begin using the Windows SIM, you should take a look at a sample answer file. Included with the ADK for Windows 8.1 is a sample `Autounattend.xml` file located in the `C:\Program Files (x86)\Windows Kits\8.1\Assessment and Deployment Kit\Deployment Tools\Samples\Unattend` folder. The sample files provided include all of the settings that are needed to automate Windows installation. Unfortunately, there is no sample available for Windows 10 at the time of going to print.

When configuring the answer file you will add the various components that will configure Windows. One of the most common settings found in most answer files will relate to setting the Windows Shell Setup component. You will notice that there are two components available depending on the architecture of your machine, as follows:

- `amd64_Microsoft-Windows-Shell-Setup` for 64-bit Windows

- `x86_Microsoft-Windows-Shell-Setup` for 32-bit Windows

Select the Windows image component applicable to your destination computer and then right click the setting. When you use the Windows SIM you will notice that the available components can be applied to one or more configuration passes, as shown in Figure 1-7.

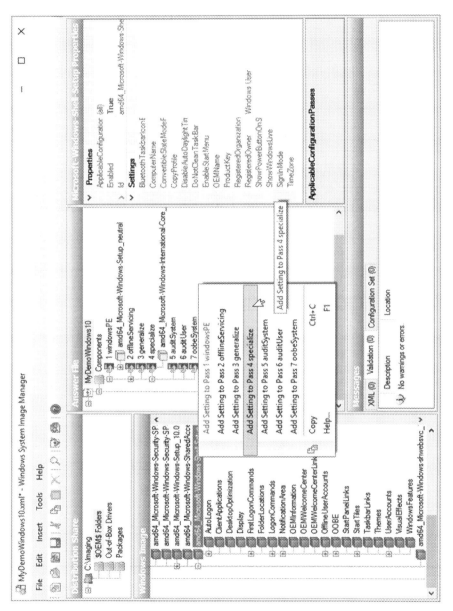

Figure 1-7. Configuring answer file settings using the Windows SIM

We learned earlier in the chapter that the Windows installation is performed via configuration passes, with four passes being used by Windows Setup. The amd64_ Microsoft-Windows-Shell-Setup component should be added to the specialize pass.

You should spend some time familiarizing yourself and experimenting with building and fine tuning an answer file using the Windows SIM.

Answer files can be used to remove much of the user interaction normally required during a Windows installation, which will then ensure an efficient and consistent deployment.

▧ **More Info**   The Windows System Image Manager Technical Reference can be found here: https://technet.microsoft.com/en-us/library/cc766347(v=ws.10).aspx

---

The Windows SIM does not modify the settings directly in a WIM file; rather, it modifies the answer file. You would use DISM to modify actual WIM files.

Windows Preinstallation Environment

Known as Windows PE or WinPE, this tool provides a lightweight version of Windows that is bootable and is often used for the deployment of Windows or for launching troubleshooting tools on a system while it is offline.

WinPE has the following functions within an enterprise setting:

- Deployment of workstations and servers

- Recovery platform to launch recovery tools

- Platform for running third-party utilities

WinPE can be booted using a USB flash drive, PXE boot on the network, a CD-ROM, or directly from a hard disk. Windows Setup, Windows Deployment Services (Windows DS), System Center Configuration Manager (SCCM), and Microsoft Deployment Toolkit (MDT) all use Windows PE to launch the deployment or capture wizards during boot time.

WinPE has been available since Windows XP and is a replacement for the MS-DOS boot disk. Originally only available to original equipment manufacturers, (OEM), the WinPE is now available within the Windows AIK and ADK. The versions and availability of WinPE are shown in Table 1-4.

Table 1-4. *Windows Preinstallation Environment Major Versions*

Version	Description and Code Base
1.0	Lightweight version of Windows XP
2.0	Built from the first edition of Windows Vista
3.0	Built from Windows 7 and included in the AIK version 2.0
4.0	Built from Windows 8 and included in the Windows ADK for Windows 8.0
5.0	Built from Windows 8.1 and included in the Windows ADK for Windows 8.1
10.0.10240	Built from the Windows 10 and included in the Windows ADK (Windows Kits 10)

▓ **More Info**   You can find more information on the WinPE: Create USB Bootable drive TechNet page: `https://technet.microsoft.com/library/hh825109.aspx`

After you have installed the ADK for Windows 10, you can create a bootable WinPE USB flash drive by following these instructions:

1. Launch the Deployment and Imaging Tools Environment.

2. At the Deployment and Imaging Tools Environment command prompt, type `copype.cmd x86 c:\winpe_x86`.

3. Install Windows PE onto the USB flash drive, specifying the appropriate drive letter using the following command: `MakeWinPEMedia /UFD C:\WinPE_x86 G:`.

You should now be able to boot to the USB flash drive, and Windows PE should load the command window.

▓ **Note**   The Makewinpemedia command-line tool is new for Windows 8 and later. The tool simplifies the creation of bootable Windows Preinstallation Environment (Windows PE) media.

Deployment Image Servicing and Management

The Deployment Image Servicing and Management (DISM) command-line tool offers administrators new functionality to prepare, service, and manage Windows images. DISM has consolidated and improved many existing or deprecated tools, such as ImageX, that are used when working with WIM files. DISM replaces PEimg, Intlcfg, and Package Manager, which were distributed with the Windows OEM Preinstallation Kit (Windows OPK) for Windows 7.

DISM can be used install, uninstall, configure, and update Windows features, packages, drivers, and international settings within offline Windows image (`.wim`) files or virtual hard disks (VHD).

Some of the DISM servicing commands can also be used to service an online operating system.

In addition to being available as part of the ADK, DISM is installed on Windows 8.1 and later and can be used to service the following Windows environments:

- Windows 10, Windows 8.1, Windows 8, Windows 7

- Windows Server 2012 R2, Windows Server 2012

- Windows Server 2008 R2, Windows Server 2008 SP2

- Windows PE 10.0, Windows PE 5.0, Windows PE 4.0 and Windows PE 3.0

In addition to the command-line tool, there are over 20 DISM cmdlets available in the DISM PowerShell module.

▓ **More Info**   You can find more information on the DISM-Deployment Image Servicing and Management Technical Reference for Windows TechNet page: `https://technet.microsoft.com/library/hh824821.aspx`

Windows Imaging and Configuration Designer

The Windows Imaging and Configuration Designer (ICD) is a new feature available in the ADK for Windows 10. In Chapter 4 you will learn how to use enterprise tools such as Microsoft Deployment Toolkit (MDT), which allows you to customize nearly every component of Windows and its deployment within a large organization. The ICD allows you to provision components, updates, and apps onto an online (running) or offline Windows 10 system without the need to reimage the device or use an enterprise tool such as MDT or System Center Configuration Manager (SCCM).

The ICD allows you to perform the following tasks:

- Create a provisioning package that can be used to update or modify devices without fully reimaging them

- Customize an existing Windows 10 image to be used for specific purposes or locations, such as installing language packs or apps

- Works with both online and offline images

The ability to deploy a provisioning package rather than needing to deploy the entire Windows image allows the more efficient use of network bandwidth and results in quicker deployments and more flexible provisioning without the investment of learning complex tools such as MDT or SCCM.

The packages (with a `.ppkg` file extension) can configure single or multiple configurations.

Examples of scenarios when you could use provisioning packages include:

- Installing or uninstalling applications, including traditional apps and modern apps

- Adding or enrolling certificates; for example, to join a secure wireless network

- Enrolling a device in corporate mobile device management (MDM) policies

- Upgrading Windows

- Configuration of bring your own device (BYOD) with corporate features such as Work Folders

Once you have installed the ADK for Windows 10, you can review the available settings and create a new provisioning package using the following steps:

1. From the Start Menu, click "All apps" and open Windows Kits, then select Windows Imaging and Configuration Designer.

2. In the Windows Imaging and Configuration Designer screen click "New provisioning package."

3. On the New Project screen, provide a project name, project folder, and option description and click Next.

4. On the New Project screen, click Next and then click Finish.

5. On the Available Customizations screen, expand and review the two nodes: Deployment Assets and Runtime Settings.

6. Under the Available Customizations, expand Runtime Settings and navigate to the ConnectivityProfiles\WiFiSense node, as shown in Figure 1-8.

7. Disable the WiFiSenseAllowed option. The setting is shown in the Selected Customizations section on the right pane.

8. You can add more settings to the provisioning package as required. Once finished, click Save on the File menu.

9. Explore the options on the menu to export or deploy the provisioning package.

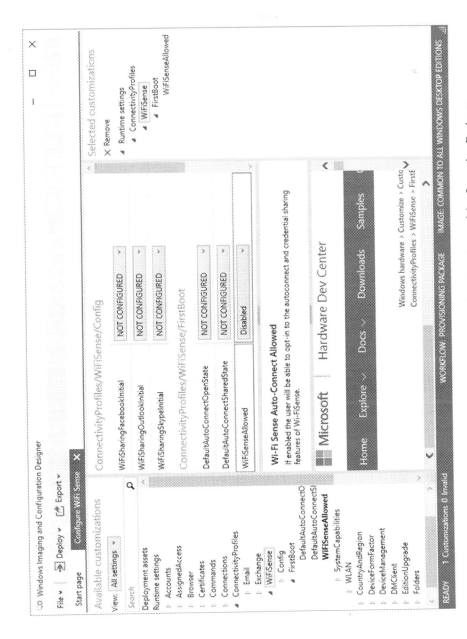

Figure 1-8. *Customizing a provisioning package with the Windows Imaging and Configuration Designer*

If you export the customization, the ICD tool will generate a file with a provisioning package (.ppkg) file extension, which can be distributed the system that requires the package. You can deploy directly within the ICD to a USB drive or a removable drive, or export the provisioning package, which can then be made available across the network or issued as an email attachment.

The provisioning package includes two files, a .ppkg file and a digitally signed catalog file (.cat). Both files must be present when the package is distributed and installed.

░ **Note**   ICD packages can be configured to apply to Windows desktop or mobile editions, Windows 10 IoT Core devices, or all Windows editions.

Upon receipt of the two files, the user will launch the .ppkg file and provide administrative credentials. After the confirmation prompt shown in Figure 1-9, the provisioning package will silently install.

Figure 1-9. Installing a provisioning package created with the ICD

░ **More Info**   You can learn more about the new ICD with the "Getting Started with Windows ICD" guide here: https://msdn.microsoft.com/ library/windows/hardware/ dn916112%28v=vs.85%29.aspx

---

If you want to script the provisioning of packages, you should use the Windows ICD (icd.exe) command-line tool.

Windows Assessment Toolkit

The Windows Assessment Toolkit allows you to test, monitor, diagnose, and report on Windows with regard to performance, reliability, and functionality. You can also focus the assessment on single or multiple sets of components.

This is useful when evaluating why a driver or app is not functioning properly. The Windows Assessment Toolkit is highly regarded as a very accurate testing tool, and it is typically used by the helpdesk, OEMs, and ISVs and can be installed on Windows 8 and later.

The toolkit includes three components:

- Windows Assessment Console

- Assessments

- Assessment Platform

By using the Windows Assessment Toolkit, you can configure and then run performance assessments within the GUI console on a variety of system components, such as battery life, browsing experience, and hardware performance. Each assessment can run for between five minutes and several hours and consists of various preconfigured performance jobs that can be created, run, viewed, and managed within the tool and be run together on the device under testing. The Windows Assessment Console displaying the battery life during connected standby assessment is shown in Figure 1-10.

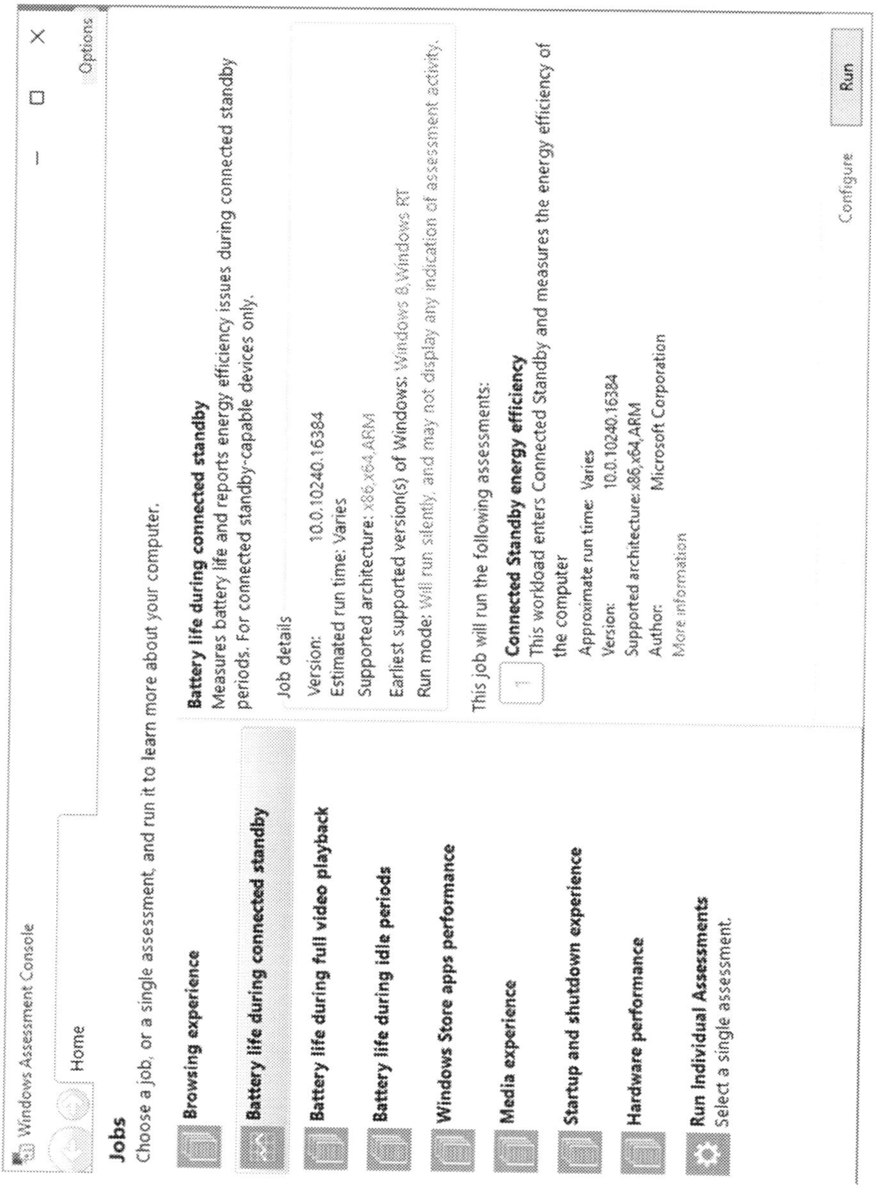

Figure 1-10. *The Windows Assessment Console*

After the tests have been performed, the results obtained can include diagnostics and remediation information, which are useful when determining areas that need additional investigation or changes to the system.

Once jobs have been created in the Windows Assessment Console, you can use the command line to run jobs using the axe.exe command-line tool. Using this tool will give you the following benefits:

- There is reduced system overhead through not using the GUI.

- There is less impact on performance metrics.

- Running a job at the command prompt uses fewer resources and has less impact on performance metrics.

- You can automate a job using axe.exe.

- Additional options and parameters are available when using axe.exe.

▓ **More Info**   You can learn more about the new Windows Assessment Toolkit with the "Windows Assessment Toolkit" guide here: https://msdn.microsoft.com/en-gb/library/windows/hardware/dn923543(v=vs.85).aspx

---

Windows Performance Toolkit

The Windows Performance Toolkit includes several low-level tools that will record and analyze issues on your Windows system. The Windows Performance Toolkit consists of two tools:

- Windows Performance Analyzer (WPA)

- Windows Performance Recorder (WPR)

The WPA uses results from the WPR and Windows Assessment Console and presents them as graphs and tables, allowing you to analyze system and application performance.

You would first run the WPR to capture trace information on performance criteria, which you can select on your system. You can select discrete components, such as file I/O activity and CPU usage, or use preset scenarios that can detect glitches with audio, video, the Edge browser, and more. Once you have allowed the tool to record and save the data, you then load the data into the WPA to analyze the results and display them, as shown in Figure 1-11.

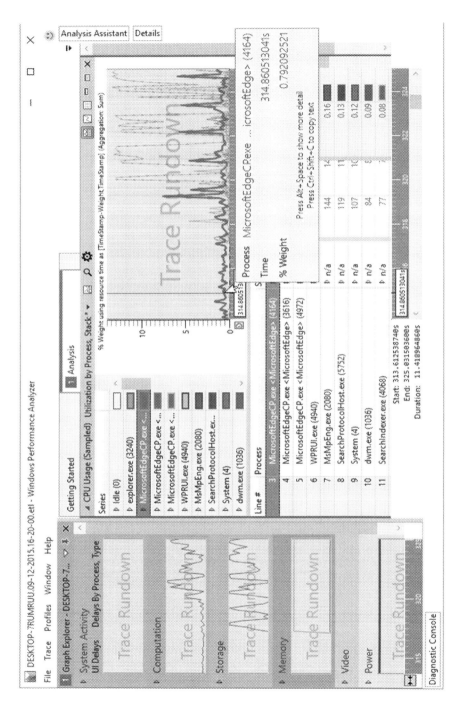

Figure 1-11. *Reviewing the performance results using Windows Performance Analyzer*

Both WPA and WPR are advanced-level tools that can be used by members of helpdesk support, developers, and independent software vendors (ISVs) to assist in troubleshooting hardware, Windows components, and application-performance issues.

░ **More Info**   You can learn more about the new Windows Performance Toolkit with the "What's New in the Windows Performance Toolkit" guide here: `https://msdn.microsoft.com/library/windows/hardware/dn927303(v=vs.85).aspx`

Summary

Schools, colleges, and enterprises are examples of organizations that need to deploy and manage a large number of desktops, laptops, and tablets. As Windows continues to grow in functionality, the underlying components contained in the operating system create more complexity when administrators need to deploy and maintain Windows.

We have seen that Microsoft effectively reinvented the method of Windows deployment with the release of Windows Vista, and the tools have continued to evolve. In this chapter you have seen that there are many tools and utilities that are available and that require careful attention; otherwise, your deployment may not go as planned.

With the introduction of the topics in this chapter, you should have a firm foundation on which the remaining chapters will build. We will focus on installing Windows locally in the next chapter.

CHAPTER 2

▓ ▓ ▓

Installing Windows Locally

The majority of PCs already have Windows preinstalled when you purchase them. Most users will never need to install Windows and will continue to use the same version of Windows for the whole lifetime of the device. Often OEMs configure their PCs with additional software, which can offer utilities and tools or trial versions of software, such as Office 2013.

Within a business environment, the experience is the opposite of that of the consumer. It is unlikely that the default installation is retained "as is," and the IT team will often replace the preinstalled version of Windows with a custom-built version that can be deployed as a complete operating system, including the business applications, drivers, and branding. This is often referred to as a Wipe and Load installation, and has been commonplace for many years.

In addition to installing Windows onto a hard drive in your computer, you can now install Windows directly into a virtual hard disk (VHD) and then provide the user the ability to boot into a choice of operating systems, including booting to the version of Windows installed into a VHD.

Virtualization allows the hosting of your operating system without worrying about the HAL or device-specific drivers. It has allowed many IT pros to build virtual machines as reference machines, which can then be sysprepped and deployed across the network. Virtualization allows for quicker and simpler deployment and testing and is often used within a corporate environment by the IT department.

In this chapter we will review the options and the tools used to install Windows locally and troubleshoot installation issues that you may encounter.

Creating Windows Installation Media (DVDs, USB, etc.)

We learned in Chapter 1 that installation media has evolved from floppy disks to CD-ROMs and DVDs, and that it is quite rare to receive any physical media when you purchase Windows nowadays. With Windows 7 it was possible to include multiple versions of Windows on the same DVD because of the use of the new Windows Image format (WIM).

© Chris Rhodes and Andrew Bettany 2016
C. Rhodes and A. Bettany, *Windows Installation and Update Troubleshooting*,
DOI 10.1007/978-1-4842-1827-3_2

If you are installing or reinstalling Windows 8.1 or Windows 10 and you do not have the installation media available, you can use the Windows Installation Media Creation Tool, shown in Figure 2-1, which will create the installation media and download it for you. This tool allows you to specify the language, edition, and architecture for the installation file and allows you to choose to save the installation file either as an ISO file or directly to a USB flash drive. You can download the tool from the following URL: `https://www.microsoft.com/en-gb/software-download/windows10` (Windows 10 version).

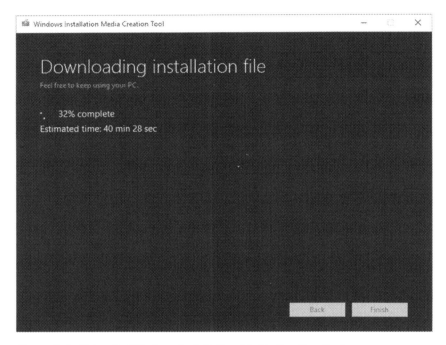

Figure 2-1. *Using the Windows Installation Media Creation Tool*

A consumer will purchase media from retail outlets, such as Best Buy or PC World. Enterprises normally access media from the Volume Licensing Service Center (VLSC), as shown in Figure 2-2, or download it from the Microsoft Developer Network (MSDN).

▓ **Note**   VLSC and MSDN Subscriptions: The MSDN subscription portal can be found at `https://msdn.microsoft.com/en-us/msdn-subscriptions-overview.aspx`. The VLSC can be found at `https://www.microsoft.com/Licensing/servicecenter/default.aspx`

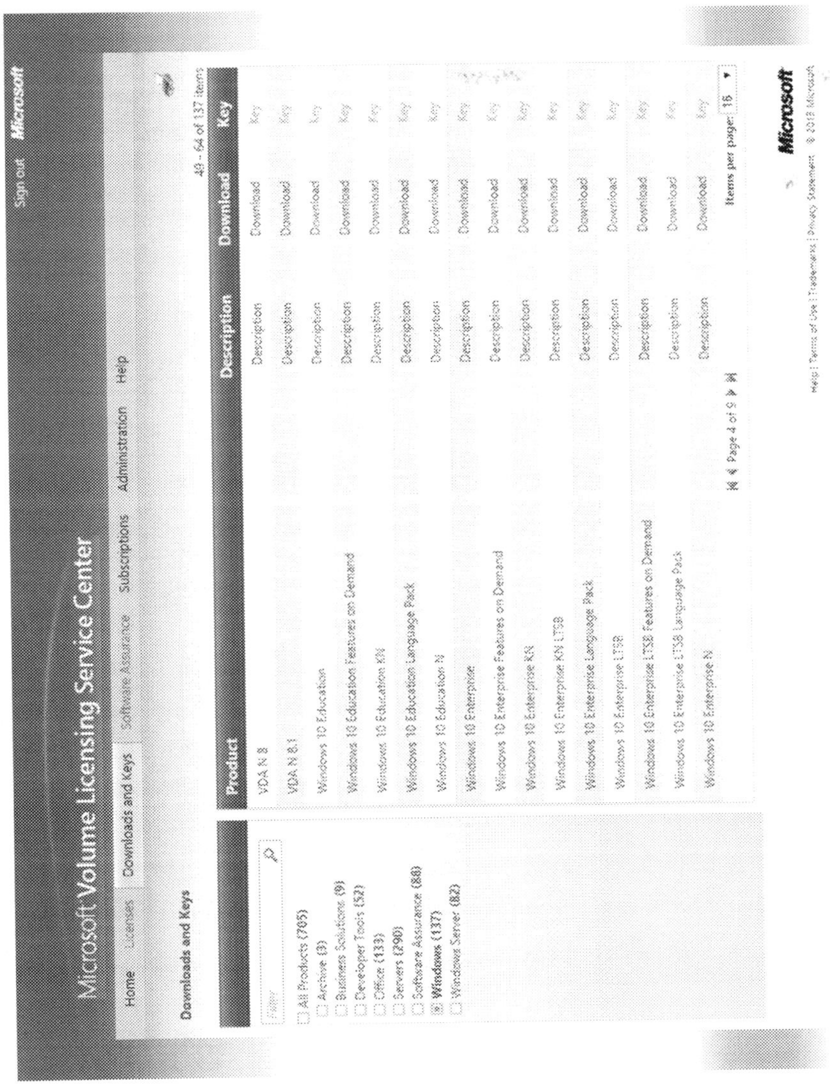

Figure 2-2. Accessing Windows builds from the VLSC

With an MSDN subscription, you are able to access over 11 terabytes of Microsoft products that have been produced by Microsoft. In addition to software and license keys to activate the software, MSDN also provides monthly Microsoft Azure cloud credit, collaboration tools, training, and support.

An enterprise will typically download the ISO image of Windows and use this with the volume license key allocated to the business as part of the VL subscription. Within the VLSC you can only download ISO images, but in the MSDN you can download ISO or VHD versions of Windows.

▓ **Note**   The VHD file size is 7613 MB for the Windows 10 Enterprise (x64) VHD, compared to the Windows 10 Enterprise (x64) ISO, which is 3757 MB in size.

You can use a VHD file directly with Hyper-V. However, you would mount an ISO image directly within File Explorer to perform an upgrade, attach it as a virtual DVD to a virtual machine, or burn it to removable media such as a DVD or USB thumb drive.

The easiest method of burning a Windows 7 or 8 image to a DVD or USB thumb drive is to use the Windows USB/DVD Download Tool, which is available free. The tool allows you to create a copy of your Windows 7 or Windows 8 ISO file on a USB thumb drive or a DVD, which is then bootable. Although not supported, this tool also works with Windows 10.

▓ **Note**   The Windows USB/DVD Download Tool is no longer available from the Microsoft Store but can be downloaded from `http://wudt.codeplex.com/`. You need to make sure that your USB stick is large enough to accommodate the Windows installation files, so it is recommended that you use a drive that is at least 8 GB in size. To create a bootable USB drive containing the Windows 10 installation files, perform the following steps:

1.   Open the Windows 7 USB/DVD Download Tool.

2.   In Step 1, browse or type the name and path of your Windows 10 ISO file and click Next.

3.   In Step 2, click USB device.

4.   In Step 3, insert your USB device and select the device in the drop-down list, then click Begin Copying.

5.   Confirm your acceptance that the USB device will be erased to allow the process to continue.

6.   In Step 4, the tool will format the drive and copy the files from the ISO file to the device.

7.   Once completed, the tool will display the message "Backup completed." You can close the tool.

The USB device will be configured to be bootable and can now be used to install Windows onto a bare metal computer or device. You may need to configure the computer to boot the USB drive within the BIOS or UEFI settings, or select the drive from a BIOS boot menu during boot up.

▦ **Note**   F8 may not work: If you have a modern PC with a UEFI BIOS and a fast SSD drive, Windows will boot so quickly that there is no time to interrupt the boot procedure with F8 or Shift F8, or for the system to display "Press F2 for Setup." On older PCs with a classic BIOS and no SSD drive, pressing these keys might still work.

If you are unable to download or use the GUI tool, you can manually create a bootable USB thumb drive using DiskPart, a command-line utility available in all modern versions of Windows and also within the Windows PE.

To create a bootable USB flash drive, follow the following steps:

1. Insert a USB flash drive into your computer.

2. Open an elevated command prompt window.

3. Type DiskPart.

4. Type list disk and press Enter.

5. All the disks on the computer should be displayed. Note the drive number or drive letter of the USB flash drive.

6. Type select disk <X>, where X is the drive number of your USB flash drive, and then press Enter.

7. Type clean, and the press Enter. This command deletes all data from the USB flash drive.

8. Type create part pri and press Enter. This creates a new primary partition on the USB flash drive.

9. Type select part 1 and then press Enter. This selects the partition that you just created.

10. To format the partition, type format fs=ntfs quick and then press Enter.

11. Type active and then press Enter. This allocates a drive letter to the drive.

12. Type exit and then press Enter to exit the DiskPart utility.

13. You can now extract all of the files in the ISO image to the root of the USB flash drive.

▓ **Note** UEFI does not support booting to NTFS USB drives. If your system uses Unified Extensible Firmware Interface (UEFI), you should format the drive as FAT32 rather than as NTFS. To format the partition as FAT32, type `format fs=fat32 quick` and then press Enter.

The Basic Input/Output System (BIOS) used to configure and initialize hardware during the booting process has been largely unchanged since the mid-1970s and offers very little protection against modern malware attacks. Unified Extensible Firmware Interface (UEFI) is the successor of BIOS and offers IT administrators significant security enhancements that protect the system from attacks on pre-boot vulnerabilities, such as rootkit infection. As we learned in Chapter 1, UEFI also provides) an abstraction layer, which allows the interface to be independent of the processor architecture.

Deploying Windows 7 and earlier editions onto a UEFI system could prove challenging, as initially there was no support for UEFI on 32-bit Windows 7. 64-bit versions of Windows supported UEFI, and Windows 8 offered optimizations that allowed systems to benefit from Secure Boot and faster boot times. Early versions of UEFI caused some compatibility issues with Secure Boot and certificates. Today, most computers are shipped with the UEFI 2.4 specification, which was finalized in April 2013 and offers improved compatibility and enhanced the UEFI 2.31 version.

Performing a Clean Installation of Windows

Now that you have created your installation media, you can perform a clean installation of Windows. You should configure your BIOS or UEFI to allow you to boot to your installation media, such as a USB drive. This can be achieved by modifying the BIOS setting or choosing a custom boot order during the boot process. Check your options onscreen during booting and select the appropriate key.

Typically, the preboot BIOS or UEFI options will offer you the ability to change the boot priority order. You should consult your motherboard manufacturer to confirm how to modify your boot menu. Keys such as DEL, F2, and ESC are often used to invoke setup or the boot menu. An example of the boot priority order listing is as follows:

- Hard drive
- USB hard drive
- CD/DVD
- USB CD/DVD
- USB floppy
- Network

░ **Note**   If you are performing a clean installation of Windows, you should consider checking whether there is a motherboard firmware upgrade available. Firmware upgrades once Windows is installed can cause activation issues. Check the website of your motherboard manufacturer for available upgrades and instructions.

If you already have an existing Windows installation, the boot process will detect this and ask if you want to boot to the installation media. At this point, you should press any key to allow the PC to load the setup files rather than boot to the existing installation.

You should check that your computer will meet the minimum hardware requirements for the operating system. Table 2-1 shows the minimum hardware requirements for Windows 8.1 and 10.

Table 2-1. *Minimum Hardware Requirements*

Hardware Component	Windows 8/8.1	Windows 10
Processor	1 gigahertz (GHz) or faster with support for Physical Address Extension (PAE), No-eXecute (NX), and Streaming SIMD Extensions 2 (SSE2)	Same as Windows 8/8.1 (1 gigahertz (GHz) or faster processor), or system on chip (SoC)
RAM	1 gigabyte (GB) (32-bit) or 2 GB (64-bit)	
Hard disk space	16 GB (32-bit) or 20 GB (64-bit)	
Graphics card	Microsoft DirectX 9 graphics device or later with Windows Display Driver Model (WDDM) 1.0 or newer	

If you are unsure whether your processor supports NX or SSE2, you can use a Windows Sysinternals tool called Coreinfo, a command-line tool that will create an output of your system CPU and memory topology, as shown in Figure 2-3.

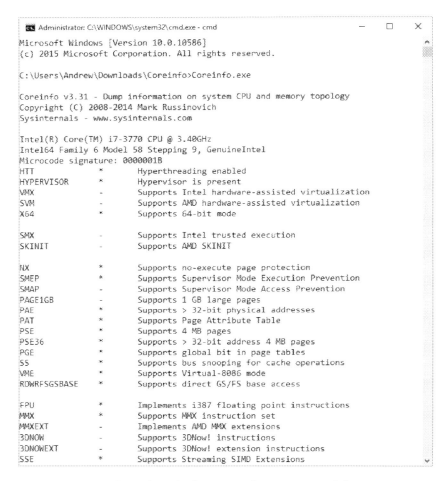

Figure 2-3. *Using Coreinfo to check processor feature compatability*

▓ **More Info**   You can download Coreinfo v3.31 from `https://technet.microsoft.com/en-us/sysinternals/cc835722`

There are several ways in which a clean installation of Windows can be performed, as shown in Table 2-2.

Table 2-2. *Windows Installation Methods*

Installation Method	Description
Install from DVD	You can use the installation media provided with a retail copy of the operating system, or you can burn an installation media obtained from MVLS or MSDN to optical media. This installation method is the slowest method.
Install from USB	Used to install on one computer at a time. Installation from a USB device is quicker than using a DVD. You must modify BIOS or UEFI settings to allow booting from USB.
Install from Windows Deployment Server (DS)	Requires Windows DS and Dynamic Host Configuration Protocol (DHCP) on a Windows-based server on the network. Target computer network card must support Pre-Boot Execution Environment (PXE). Windows DS allows the automated installation of system images and the deployment of Windows to multiple computers simultaneously using multicast.
Install an image from Windows Preinstallation Environment (PE)	Boot the device using Windows Preinstallation Environment (PE) and then use one of the following deployment options: Use Deployment Image Servicing and Management (DISM) to apply the Windows image Use the Microsoft Deployment Toolkit (MDT) deployment solution Use the System Center 2012 R2 Configuration Manager (SCCM) deployment solution Both MDT and SCCM are enterprise-level solutions that allow you to deploy Windows to hundreds or thousands of devices at once and allow you to configure lite-touch installation (LTI) and zero-touch installation (ZTI), which allow either minimal user interaction or no user interaction during the deployment.
Install over the network	Start the computer by using Windows PE and connect to a copy of the installation files stored on a shared network folder. You would use this method when you are unable to utilize a USB device, Windows DS, MDT, or Configuration Manager.

During a clean installation on a new hard drive, you should perform the following steps to install Windows 8.1:

1. Insert the installation media that contains Windows 8.1 and boot the computer to load it.

2. When the Windows Setup screen appears, choose the appropriate regional settings, then click Next.

3. In the Windows Setup window, click Install.

4. On the License Terms page, select the "I accept the license terms" checkbox and then click Next.

5. On the Which Type of Installation Do You Want? page, click Custom: Install Windows Only (advanced).

6. On the Where Do You Want to Install Windows? page, click Next.

Windows will now install and the following stages will be performed:

- Copying Windows files

- Getting files ready for installation

- Installing features

- Installing updates

- Finishing up

Depending on your hardware performance, Windows should complete the process within 15 to 20 minutes, and the machine will reboot several times. Once Windows has completed the installation, you will be presented with the Personalize and then the Settings welcome pages in Windows 8.1, or the Get Going Fast page if you install Windows 10.

▓ **Note**　If you are installing Windows on a machine that already has an operating system installed, you will need to erase the partition that you intend to install Windows on, and therefore you must ensure that all data and settings that you want to retain are backed up prior to deleting the partition.

If the Windows installation fails to complete, you should consider the following issues and possible remedies:

- Corrupt ISO image – download a new ISO image

- Faulty installation media, such as a corrupt DVD – try burning the DVD at a slower speed

- Drive controller issues – update the firmware

- Drive corruption – fix drive errors or replace the drive

- RAM memory errors – click the "Repair your computer" link and run the built-in Memory Diagnostics tool

- Motherboard firmware corruption or incompatibility – update the firmware

When faced with installation failure issues you should troubleshoot the problem to find the cause and then replace the corruption or failed component. You can also use the Startup Repair recovery tool if there is an issue or corruption with the boot process once Windows has been installed.

Migrating to a New Version of Windows (USMT, Easy Transfer)

Windows allows users and system administrators to migrate the user state, which contains the data and settings, from one computer and apply them to another computer. This is especially advantageous when you have many customized settings and files that are stored locally on the source computer.

You must first decide which type of migration scenario you are using, as follows:

- Side-by-side migration – This method migrates the information from the source computer and applies it to the new computer. The migration files can be stored in an intermediate store on another computer, such as a file server on the network.

- In-place migration – In this scenario the source computer is refreshed with the new operating system and the user state from the original operating system is then applied to the new installation. This is also known as a wipe-and-load or refresh scenario.

Both of the migration scenarios require a clean installation of Windows.

A migration provides the user with a clean installation, which can be used to provide a newer operating system to the user while retaining most if not all of the customized Windows and application settings. By offering a clean install, all previous files and any potential harmful malware or obsolete file "clutter" on the computer will be removed, which can enhance the performance and productivity of the device.

In an upgrade operation all of the user files, settings, and applications are retained, which is beneficial to the end user because the loss of productivity is minimized. With a clean installation and migration scenario, the process is more complicated and could be more time consuming, because a migration will typically require the reinstallation of applications and the reconfiguration of applications and settings.

Microsoft provides two tools for you to use when performing a migration, as follows:

- Windows Easy Transfer (WET) – This is a GUI tool that can be used with Windows 7 or Windows 8 (it is not available with Windows 10). The WET tool is built into Windows and can found by searching for Windows Easy Transfer on the Start screen. WET can also be installed onto a down-level operating system, such as Windows 7, from the Windows 8 installation media. For Windows 8.1, you can still use WET to import settings but not to export them.

- User State Migration Tool (USMT) – This is useful for larger projects and is a command-line scriptable tool that can be used with all versions of Windows. The USMT is part of the Windows Assessment and Deployment Kit (ADK) for Windows 10; more information about the Windows ADK can be found at `https://msdn.microsoft.com/en-us/windows/hardware/dn913721.aspx?f=255&MSPPError=-2147217396`

You will learn about advanced deployment tools later in this book, and you should know that when you use the Microsoft Deployment Toolkit (MDT), USMT is integrated into MDT and can be used as part of the deployment and migration process.

USMT uses three command-line tools, with the ScanState and LoadState tools being the most important:

- `ScanState.exe` – for performing the user-state backup

- `LoadState.exe` – for performing the user-state restore

- `UsmtUtils.exe` – adds support for directory and cryptographic options and for your migration

USMT supports migrating from a 32-bit architecture to a 64-bit operating system. For example, you can use USMT to migrate from Windows 7 x86 to Windows 10 x64.

USMT will migrate data contained in the user profile and also settings contained in Control Panel configurations and file types. The configuration settings are stored in templates that are used by USMT. For Windows 10 deployments, the two default templates are `MigUser.xml` and `MigApp.xml`, which will migrate the following data and settings:

- Folders from each profile, including user profiles and shared and public profiles (including My Documents, My Video, My Music, My Pictures, desktop files, Start menu, Quick Launch settings, and Favorites folders)

- Specific file types

- Operating system component settings

- Application settings

The overview steps that need to be performed in any migration scenario include the following:

1. Back up your computer.

2. Save user settings and data for migration (WET or ScanState.exe).

3. Install Windows using a clean installation.

4. Reinstall applications.

5. Restore user settings and data (WET or LoadState.exe).

▓ **Note** Once the migration data and settings have been captured using ScanState.exe, it is important that any applications you want the retained settings applied to are installed onto the new computer prior to using LoadState.exe.

There are many third-party migration tools that offer enhanced functionality when performing migrations; for example, some of the following tools offer the ability to rejoin computers to the domain, allow push migrations, and provide GUI support for migrating to Windows 10. Some tools available are listed in Table 2-3. These tools often allow a free trial version, but if you want to use them in a professional environment you will need to purchase the appropriate license.

Table 2-3. *Some Thied-Party Migration Tools (Paid)*

Tool	URL	Description
User Profile Wizard	http://www.forensit.com/domain-migration.html	Offers user profile migrations, including domain join and VPN capability
Zinstall Easy Transfer	http://www.zinstall.com/products/zinstall-easy-transfer	GUI tool that migrates files and settings. Works with Windows XP, Vista, 7, 8, and 10
Zinstall WinWin	http://www.zinstall.com/products/zinstall-winwin	GUI tool that migrates applications in addition to files and settings. Works with Windows XP, Vista, 7, 8, and 10
CloneApp	http://www.mirinsoft.com/	Creates a backup of your app settings from the Windows directories and the Registry, which can then be reinstated on the new machine
PCmover	http://www.laplink.com	GUI tool that migrates applications, files, and settings; works with Windows XP, Vista, 7, and 8

Managing the Windows Boot Partitions and Files

The boot and system partitions are the volumes on a hard disk that Windows uses to start and load the operating system. The terms are quite old and relate to the earliest days of computing. Unfortunately, when you try to learn what each partition contains, it can be confusing, and you may think Table 2-4 contains the wrong information.

Table 2-4. *System and Boot Partition Contents*

Partition	Contents	Notes
System	Files required to boot Windows	The Boot folder contains files that start Windows, including the Windows Boot Manager (BootMgr).
		Only ever have one system partition on a computer running Windows.
		The files found in the active partition are used to determine the operating system used to start the computer.
Boot	Contains system files	The boot partition contains Windows operating system files.
		In a multiboot scenario, each version of Windows will be stored on a separate volume containing the respective Windows operating system files.

We will see later in this section that it is essential that you can identify the correct partition, as you can cause the device to be unbootable if you mix the partitions.

There are several ways for you to identify which partition is the boot or system, such as using PowerShell, Disk Management, and BCDEdit. We will use the Disk Management snap-in to view this information using the following the steps:

1. Search for and open Disk Management.

2. Expand the width of the Status column.

3. You should now see the status of the partitions, and the drive letters if provided.

4. The system partition is indicated by (System) (no drive letter, in our example).

5. The boot partition is indicated by (Boot) (C: drive in our example, as shown in Figure 2-4).

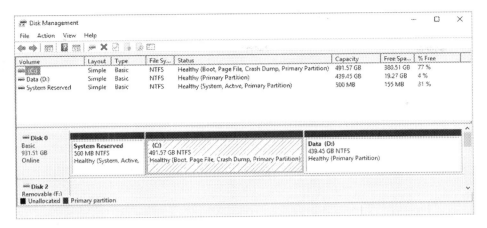

Figure 2-4. Disk Management displaying boot and system partitions

To list the system partition using PowerShell, you can use the following cmdlet: `Get-Volume -FileSystemLabel "System Reserved"`

The configuration parameters for loading Windows are stored in the Boot Configuration Data (BCD) store. The primary tool for working with the actual boot records is the command-line tool BCD Editor (`Bcdedit.exe`). Great care should be exercised when modifying the boot records, as misconfiguration can lead to an unstable or non-bootable device.

To view the contents of your boot configuration, use the following steps:

1. Open an elevated command prompt or administrative PowerShell console.

2. Type `BCDEdit /v` and then press Enter.

3. Review the output.

If you have a multiple -boot system, the output should be similar to the contents of Figure 2-5.

Figure 2-5. *Using BCDEdit to view the boot configuration*

In Figure 2-5, you should see two sections: a Windows Boot Manager and a Windows Boot Loader. The descriptions of the boot entries are shown as Windows 8.1 and Microsoft Windows 10. Each operating system found in the boot configuration database will have its own globally unique identifier (GUID). In the example shown in Figure 2-5, the two GUIDs are as follows:

- Windows 8.1: {37e47a93-6808-11e5-b2f0-83e8e58e54e8}

- Microsoft Windows 10: {37e47a8f-6808-11e5-b2f0-83e8e58e54e8}

Note that there is a third entry for an Ubuntu installation, with the GUID of {37e47a99-6808-11e5-b2f0-83e8e58e54e8}, but this entry has scrolled off the screen.

If you want to change the displayed name of the operating system setting, you can use the following command:

BCDEdit /set {GUID} description "OS Name"

Substitute the GUID placeholder for the Windows Boot Loader identifier (GUID) found in the Windows Boot Loader entry that you want to change.

░ **Note**   If you have multiple boot sectors, these will be listed using the BCDEdit tool. For non-Windows entries, this will be listed with a section heading named "Real-mode Boot Sector."

Multi-Booting Windows

Multi-booting a computer allows you to install multiple operating systems on the same computer. You may want to run Windows 7 as your main business operating system and also use Windows 10 for home use or testing while you evaluate it or become comfortable with the new operating system.

Multi-booting Windows can be useful in certain specialist cases, such when users share a device and each user requires a different operating system. The main reasons for using a dual-boot configuration are as follows:

- Testing a new operating system – This is the most common use for a multi-boot configuration. New operating systems, especially when in the beta or preview phase, are often incomplete or contract bugs or compatibility issues with hardware and software. By multi-booting the new OS and test driving it on the physical hardware, you can evaluate to see if it is compatible with your existing hardware while retaining the full functionality of the device, which can be booted back to the original operating system.

- Testing application compatibility – Often your current or legacy applications may not be compatible with a new operating system. Issues with compatibility can force you to delay or even to not upgrade your version of Windows. You should therefore establish a system of testing the application compatibility as soon as possible and report problems to your own development team or the independent software vendor (ISV) so that they can begin to resolve issues early.

- Multiple users – A multi-boot situation can allow one computer to be used with multiple users, with either the same operating system version or different versions installed. Example usage cases include shift workers working at different times of the day on a single PC, users requiring specialist or legacy applications that rely on an older operating system, or software requiring access to older hardware or peripherals. Of course, there are other more modern methods of sharing a PC among multiple users, such as using different user accounts.

We will cover the use of Hyper-V and booting to VHD–which offer users modern alternatives to multi booting–later in this chapter, but we should appreciate that there are numerous users who are very much still operating a multi-boot scenario, either at home or in a business environment.

The process for creating a multi-boot environment must start with proper planning and precautions. You should ensure that you either have a full backup of your computer or use a test lab to perform the operation.

To multi-boot Windows with any other operating system, you should first install the newest version of Windows that is available on the computer.

In order to keep the two operating systems logically separate, you need to have at least two partitions on your computer. If you do not have a spare partition, you may need to create one, and that could involve shrinking your current operating system partition to free up space. This is performed using a third-party tool, or by using built-in tools such as DiskPart or Disk Management. To use Disk Management to create a second partition on which to install Windows in a multi-boot environment, follow these steps:

1. Type `diskmgmt.msc` into the Search box or Run command and then press Enter.

2. Locate the primary partition, which is marked as (`Boot, Page File, Crash Dump, Primary Partition`) and is normally your C: drive.

3. Right click the C: drive and select Shrink Volume.

4. In the Shrink C: dialog box, enter the size in MB that you want to shrink the drive, such as 40960 MB, as shown in Figure 2-6, and click Shrink.

5. The 40.00 GB partition will be formatted by the Windows installation program. Close Disk Management.

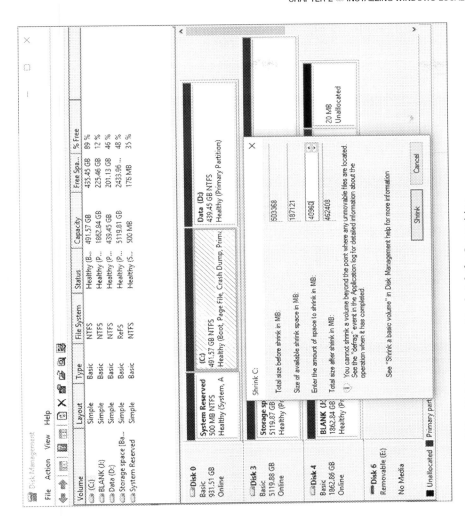

***Figure 2-6.** Using Disk Management to shrink the C: partition*

The next stage in creating a dual-boot environment is to install the second operating system onto the newly created partition, as follows:

1. Insert your installation media, such as a DVD or bootable USB drive.

2. Reboot your system and press any key when the system detects the bootable USB drive or DVD.

3. After the setup program loads, proceed with the setup as for a clean installation and select the newly created Unallocated Space (the 40.0 GB drive in the preceding example) as the location in which to install Windows, then click Next.

4. Allow the Windows installation to complete and then configure the additional version of Windows.

5. To switch between the two operating systems, you will need to reboot your system and choose the desired version of Windows in the boot menu.

6. On the Choose an Operating System boot menu, if you click the "Change defaults or choose other options" link you will be presented with the Options screen, as shown in Figure 2-7.

7. In the Options menu you can choose how long the onscreen prompt will be visible and which operating system you want to boot by default, and also access repair tools.

Figure 2-7. The Options menu displaying dual-boot configuration options

If you can't live without using the F8 key to bring up the Advanced Options menu, which is disabled in Windows 8 and newer (though it is still present in Windows Server 2012 and newer), you can modify the boot manager to revert to the legacy (F8) setting as follows:

1. Launch an administrative command prompt.

2. Type BCDEdit /set {default} bootmenupolicy legacy and press Enter.

3. Reboot your system.

4. Try to press F8 during booting; the Advanced Options menu should now appear.

5. To reset the system to the default, repeat Step 1 and type BCDEdit /set {default} bootmenupolicy standard.

There are many third-party tools that can be used to simplify the process of dual-booting Windows. Often the vendor will allow a free trial to evaluate the tool; for enterprise usage you should purchase the applicable license. Some of these tools are listed in Table 2-5.

Table 2-5. *Some Third-Party Dual-Boot Tools*

Tool	URL	Description
Acronis Disk Director 12	http://www.acronis.com/en-us/personal/disk-manager/	Create and manage disk partitions to store different file systems or operating systems on one disk
EasyBCD	http://neosmart.net/EasyBCD/	Provides GUI tool to dual-boot Windows, Linux, Mac, and Unix. Boot from and into USB drives, ISO images, virtual disks, and more. Windows 10 compatible
BootIt Bare Metal	http://www.terabyteunlimited.com/bootit-bare-metal.htm	Manage your partitions; install and boot multiple operating systems
DualBootPRO	http://www.dualbootpro.org/	Allows manipulation and editing of the Boot Configuration Data (BCD) store and includes built-in diagnostics to help find and correct errors in the BCD store

Installing a Non-Windows OS, Such as Linux/MAC

Linux can run from just a USB drive without your configuring your system. If you plan to use Linux often you can install it on your PC alongside Windows as a "multi-boot," which will give you a choice of either operating system each time you boot your PC.

To multi-boot with Windows and Linux, you must install Linux on your PC after Windows has already been installed. First, you need to download the version of Linux that you want to install. In the following example I have used Ubuntu LTS, which requires 1006 MB and can be downloaded as an ISO from http://www.ubuntu.com/download/desktop.

▓ **Note**   Windows should always be installed first. If you install Windows after Linux, Windows will ignore the Linux installation and will overwrite the Linux boot loader with the Windows version. Always install Windows first and then Linux.

With a modern version of Linux, the process of setting up dual booting is quite straightforward and painless. The steps are as follows:

1. Boot your Windows PC to a USB drive or DVD containing your Linux distribution.

2. At the GNU GRUB screen select Install Ubuntu.

3. Choose the option to install Ubuntu alongside Windows, as shown in Figure 2-8, and do not choose the option that will overwrite your Windows system with Linux.

4. Allow Ubuntu to install.

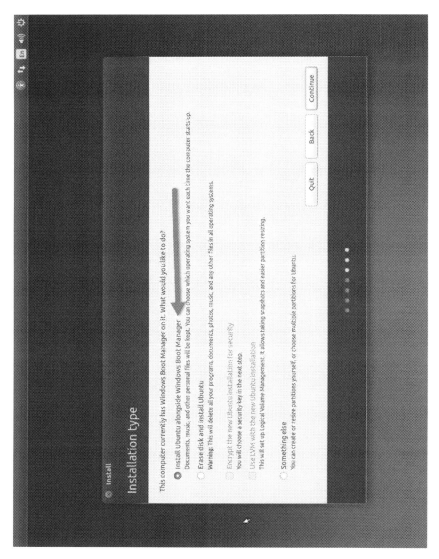

Figure 2-8. *Installing Ubuntu alongside Windows*

Once Ubuntu has been installed, you can select Linux or Windows from the boot menu by using the arrow keys and the Enter key.

If you want to view your files stored on a Windows partition, most Linux distributions allow you access in your Linux desktop file manager. Windows does not natively provide easy access to the Linux ext4 file system, however. You can install a third-party file-explorer driver that supports ext4 file systems on your Windows machine if you require that functionality.

Examples of Windows file-system drivers that support Linux file systems include Ext2Fsd, Linux Reader from DiskInternals, and Ext2explore.

If you encounter problems with the boot loader or Linux not appearing in your boot menu, you can try one of the following troubleshooting options:

- Boot to a Windows Recovery environment and choose "start up repair," or type `Bootrec.exe /fixmbr` into an elevated command prompt.

- Use the EasyBCD third-party tool to create a Linux entry in your boot menu.

- Use the Ubuntu live-CD, live-USB, or Ubuntu installation media and boot to Linux, then download and install the Boot-Repair tool within Ubuntu.

- If you are using Hyper-V, modify the boot order within the firmware settings to prioritize booting the `shimx64.efi` boot loader.

VHD Boot

If you are not confident with dual booting, or if you would like to run another operating system within a virtual hard disk (VHD), you can using VHD Boot. VHD Boot is still relatively new and is thought of as being quite specialist. Instead of installing the operating system directly onto the physical hard drive, you prepare a virtual hard drive first and then install the operating system directly onto this, fooling Windows into thinking it is a normal drive during the installation process.

To create a VHD and configure it so that you can install Windows, you should follow these steps:

1. Type `diskmgmt.msc` into the search area or right click the Start button and click Disk Management.

2. In Disk Management click Action, then click Create VHD.

3. On the Create and Attach Virtual Hard Disk dialog box, provide the parameters for your VHD. An example VHD would be:

    a. Location: `C:\VHD\Windows10vhd.vhd`

    b. Virtual hard disk size: 40 GB

    c. Virtual hard disk format: VHD

    d. Virtual hard disk type: Fixed size

4. Click OK to create your VHD. Because we selected fixed type, this may take several minutes to complete, and you will see the creation progress in the bottom right of the Disk Management dialog box.

5. Once created, your new VHD should automatically be attached to the system, but if not, use Disk Management to attach the drive as follows: Click Action, then click Attach VHD, browse to your new VHD, and choose the VHD to attach.

6. If you prefer to use the command line, you could also use the DiskPart tool and type `create vdisk file= C:\VHD\ Windows10vhd.vhd maximum=40960 type=fixed` to achieve the same result.

7. Leave the VHD drive in the Not Initialized state; this will be updated once Windows installs to it.

8. You are now ready to install Windows into your VHD file.

To install Windows inside your VHD file, you should follow these steps:

1. Insert your Windows media (or ISO if you are using a Virtual Machine) into your computer and boot from it.

2. Follow the onscreen prompts, providing the appropriate information until the Where Do You Want to Install Windows? screen appears.

3. Press Shift+F10, which will launch an administrative command prompt window.

4. In the administrative command prompt window type `DiskPart`.

5. In DiskPart, type `List disk`.

6. Locate the VHD disk that you have created and type `select vdisk file=D:\VHD\Windows10vhd.vhd` (notice the drive letter has been changed).

7. In DiskPart, type `attach vdisk` and press Enter.

8. Type `Exit` to close DiskPart and then close the administrative command prompt window.

9. In the Where Do You Want to Install Windows? screen, click Refresh, and your VHD disk should now appear.

10. Select the VHD drive and allow Windows to install normally.

11. Upon completion, after rebooting the machine, you should see the ability to choose an operating system during boot time, as shown in Figure 2-9.

Figure 2-9. Choosing an operating system to dual boot

Installing Windows in Hyper-V

Hyper-V has been available for several years and has improved steadily against its arch rival VMware. One huge advantage for Microsoft in driving awareness (and adoption) is that Hyper-V is bundled into the business editions of Windows 8 and later and offers you a production-class virtualization tool.

Your hardware needs the following characteristics to support virtualization using Hyper-V:

- Windows 8 Pro or Enterprise or newer

- 64-bit architecture

- 64-bit processor with Second Level Address Translation (SLAT)

- Minimum of 4 GB system RAM

- BIOS/UEFI-level hardware virtualization support

The ability to test and evaluate other operating systems within a sandboxed virtualized environment is so much quicker (and easier) once you have an understanding of virtualization and Hyper-V.

In this last section of this chapter, we will provide detailed steps for you to follow to install Windows 10 Enterprise Evaluation within a Hyper-V virtual machine, as follows:

1. Download the Windows 10 Enterprise Evaluation ISO from
   `https://www.microsoft.com/en-us/evalcenter/evaluate-`
   `windows-10-enterprise`.

2. Launch Programs and Features from the administrative menu on the Start button.

3. Click Turn Windows Features On or Off.

4. Enable the Hyper-V feature by placing a tick next to Hyper-V, as shown in Figure 2-10.

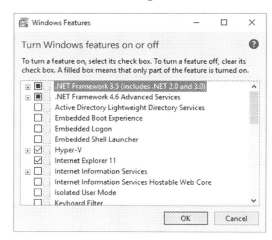

Figure 2-10. *Naming your Hyper-V virtual machine*

5.   Reboot Windows to complete the configuration of Hyper-V.

6.   Launch Hyper-V by typing Hyper-V into the Start menu or searching for Hyper-V.

7.   To create a virtual machine, in the Actions pane click New > Virtual Machine.

8.   On the Before You Begin screen, click Next.

9.   On the Specify Name and Location screen, enter the desired name for the VM.

10.   Modify the location to store the VM to be a location such as D\ VMs\ and click Next, as shown in Figure 2-11.

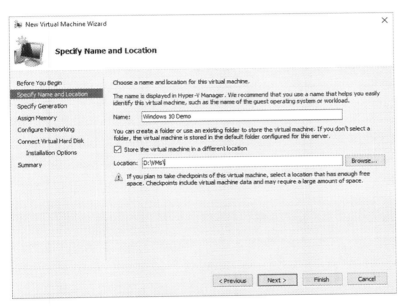

Figure 2-11. *Hyper-V virtual machine beginning Windows 10 installation*

11.   On the Specify Generation screen, select Generation 1 and click Next.

12.   On the Assign Memory screen, enter a memory size, such as 2048 MB, ignore the Dynamic Memory option, and click Next.

13. On the Configure Networking screen, select a suitable
    network connection or select Not Connected and click Next.

14. On the Connect Virtual Hard Disk page, select Create a Virtual
    Hard Disk, leave the default 127 GB dynamically expanding
    virtual hard disk settings, and click Next.

15. On the Installation Options screen, select the Install an
    Operating System from a Bootable CD/DVD-ROM option.

16. Select the Windows 10 Enterprise Evaluation image file (`.iso`)
    downloaded in Step 1 and click Next.

17. On the Completing the New Virtual Machine Wizard screen,
    review the selected options and click Finish.

18. Hyper-V will provision the virtual machine.

19. In Hyper-V Manager, right click on the newly created virtual
    machine and click Start.

20. Right click or double click on your virtual machine and click
    Connect to open the virtual machine.

21. The virtual machine will begin to install Windows 10
    Enterprise, as shown in Figure 2-12, from the ISO file, which is
    configured as a virtual DVD.

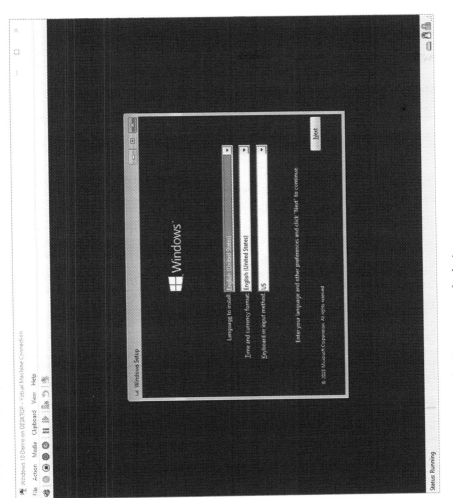

Figure 2-12. Verifying the licence status of a device

You should familiarize yourself with Hyper-V, as virtualization is an excellent tool for testing, troubleshooting, evaluating, sandboxing applications, deployment testing, and many more operations.

Some of the many benefits of using virtualization in Hyper-V include the following:

- Released in 2008 – It is a mature and well-supported platform.

- Saves time – Physical devices, especially servers, take a long time to provision, maintain, and update/patch, whereas virtualization can speed up tasks with very fast virtual hardware.

- Speed of provisioning and decommissioning – Physical hardware needs to be purchased, shipped, unboxed, and set up, whereas virtual machines can be provisioned extremely quickly.

- Ease of repetitiveness – Tasks can be automated, repeated, paused, copied, and exported.

- Secure and stable – Hyper-V utilizes a micro-kernelized hypervisor, which allows device drivers and other components to be stored in a compartmentalized fashion.

- Windows-based platform – The Hyper-V platform is Windows based, which has a familiar MMC GUI and can also be completely driven and managed by PowerShell.

Windows Activation Options (Retail, MAC, KMS, AD BA)

Microsoft has used the activation of Windows to safeguard its own intellectual property from piracy theft by proving that the user of the software has a valid software license.

Over the last 20 years, Microsoft has developed and introduced several different methods of activating software. Some are evolutions over time, while others have been available concurrently throughout this period in differing scenarios and for various types of licensed customers.

The activation process requires external validation, which can be done via one of the following validation services:

- online activation service at Microsoft

- by phone to an automated activation service at Microsoft

- through a Key Management Service

- through Active Directory Directory Services

Once the activation process has succeeded, the software key is then linked to the specific hardware of the device. You should be aware that if your hardware significantly changes, such as if you change the processor or add a new graphics card, the device may "look" like it is different than the original, and you may need to reactivate the system with Microsoft so that they can update the license record.

You should also be very careful when purchasing Windows outside of normal corporate channels. Some editions do not offer you the same functionality; for example, a Windows 8.1 DVD purchased in a big box store may not be able to join and connect to a corporate network that uses a domain. As you can imagine, it would not be appropriate or cost effective for a large organization with thousands of devices to purchase retail versions of Windows. They are able to bulk purchase keys as part of a Volume Licensing program that Microsoft operates. In most cases, a corporation will have a relationship with a software asset and licensing management partner, who will provide the most appropriate and cost-effective licensing for your business.

▓ **More Info**   For more information relating to licensing and volume activation, visit
`http://go.microsoft.com/fwlink/?LinkId=378217&clcid=0x409`

There are six types of keys available, as shown in Table 2-6.

Table 2-6. *Types of Microsoft License Keys*

Type of Key	Description
Retail license key	Software purchased at a retail store such as Best Buy (standalone or bundled with hardware) will contain one unique product key supplied on a label inside the Windows box. It can be used only once to activate the bundled software on one device. Typically, the Windows keys are 25 characters in length and are similar to this: AVFD3-2FPPP-ABY43-QR3VK-WT4CK. Some devices still carry a sticker that contains the Certificate of Authenticity (COA), which is attached to the device.
Original equipment manufacturer (OEM)	The OEM purchases a bulk amount of keys from Microsoft and allocates one key to each piece of software or hardware device. These keys are not transferrable away from the OEM device.
Key Management Service (KMS) key	Part of the Microsoft Volume Licensing program, requiring the Volume Activation Services server role to be running on a Windows Server 2012 or newer. Allows Windows 7 and newer versions to activate without needing to connect to Microsoft activation servers. KMS requires a minimum estate size of 25 client computers, or more than five servers to use KMS activation.

(continued)

Table 2-6. (*continued*)

Type of Key	Description
Active Directory–based activation	Part of the Microsoft Volume Licensing program, requiring the Volume Activation Services server role to be running on a Windows Server 2012 or newer. Allows Windows 7 and newer versions to activate without needing to connect to Microsoft activation servers. Within a domain, this method allows Active Directory Domain Services (AD DS) to store the activation status of devices, and the device remains activated so long as it remains part of the domain.
Multiple activation key (MAKs)	Obtained only as part of the Microsoft Volume Licensing program. A fixed number of activations can be made available to a MAK key. Once the activation pool has been depleted, no further device will be activated unless the MAK key is reloaded.
Digital entitlement (hardware-based key)	A new method introduced with Windows 10 that allows the hardware itself to be registered and effectively become the key. This information is recorded by Microsoft for licensing purposes so that if you need to reinstall your device at a later date, there is no need for license key entry. The computer information could be obtained from the system BIOS or UEFI configuration.

▓ **Note**   The free Windows 10 license available from Microsoft until July 2016 can be used when you are upgrading from a licensed version of Windows 7, 8, or 8.1. The upgrade process registers on Microsoft's activation servers a unique ID that is tied to your PC's hardware. Subsequent reinstalls of Windows 10 after July 2016 on the same PC will automatically be activated. You can find more information about the "Get Windows 10" promotion at the Microsoft Store here: http://www.microsoftstore.com/store/msusa/ en_US/pdp/Windows-10-Home/productID.319937100

To determine the status of a Windows 8.1 or later device, open a command prompt and type the command shown in Figure 2-13:

```
Cscript C:\windows\system32\slmgr.vbs –dli
```

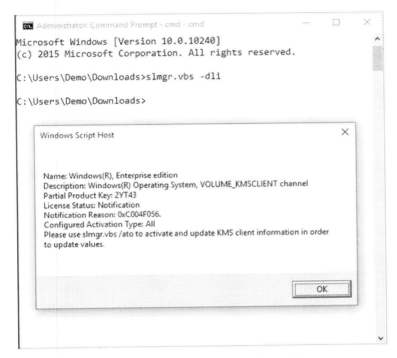

Figure 2-13. *Enable the Hyper-V feature in Windows 10*

Some editions of Windows may be able to use one or more activation methods. Table 2-7 shows the types of activation available for Windows 8.1 and Windows 10.

Table 2-7. *Activation Options Available*

Version of Windows	Activation Method	Comments
Windows 8.1	Retail license key	
Windows 8.1 Pro	Retail license key, MAK key, KMS keys	
Windows 8.1 Enterprise	MAK key, KMS keys	Volume Licensing only
Windows 8.1 evaluation edition (90 days)	No key required	Available as an ISO image from MSDN and Microsoft Partner network
Windows 10 Enterprise evaluation edition (90 days)	Key not needed	For recovery scenarios, the following key is provided: VTNMT-2FMYP-QCY43-QR9VK-WTVCK
Windows 10 Home	Digital Entitlement, retail license key	Digital Entitlement does not require you to enter a product key.
Windows 10 Pro	Digital Entitlement, MAK key, KMS keys	
Windows 10 Enterprise	MAK key, KMS keys	Volume Licensing only
Windows 10 Education	MAK key, KMS keys	Volume Licensing only

Evaluation editions of many current versions of Windows software are available at `https://www.microsoft.com/en-us/evalcenter`.

▦ **Note**   The version of Windows 10 (version 1511 or higher) can be activated using selected Windows 7, 8, and 8.1 product keys. More information can be found here: `http://windows.microsoft.com/en-us/windows-10/activation-in-windows-10`

The MAK method of activation is typically used in corporate scenarios where the devices rarely or never connect to the corporate network. There are two types of activation for MAK keys, as follows:

- Independent activation – Each device will connect to the Microsoft activation servers (via the Internet or telephone) and activate.

- MAK Proxy activation – This activates to a centralized activation proxy device, which then connects to Microsoft. An enterprise-level configuration tool called the Volume Activation Management Tool (VAMT) is used to configure the MAK Proxy.

▓ **Note** Windows 10 and 8.1 do not have a grace period. You are encouraged to activate Windows once installation has been completed, otherwise the user will be prevented from customizing the device.

Troubleshooting Activation Issues

This list features several common issues relating to activation that you may encounter:

- Take care when employees purchase OEM or retail Windows devices from computer stores, as sometimes a retail or OEM key cannot be used to join a computer to a domain, and you will need to upgrade the version of Windows to Pro or Enterprise with a new key.

- If a device is initially activated and then deployed to a remote worker, you should take care not to use a KMS key unless you expect the user to connect the device to the corporate network at least once in every 180 days; otherwise, the device will fall out of activation.

- If you use KMS, you can allow computers to use RPCs over TCP/IP using the default port of 1688 to connect to the KMS host. Ensure that this port is configured in your firewall; otherwise, activation may fail.

- Windows Server 2012 and newer are required to use AD-based activation.

- The AD DS schema must at least be at the Windows Server 2012 functional level to allow AD-based activation to operate.

- Once implemented once, AD-based activation is operational forest wide.

- MAK keys can be used accidently or carelessly; tight control and guidance of MAK Volume Licensing should be provided to ensure wasted activations do not occur.

Summary

Often, consumers will purchase devices preinstalled with Windows by the OEM, and they will have little ability to customize the experience until the OOBE stage of the Windows installation. In many environments, such as a college or enterprise where hundreds or thousands of devices are replaced or upgraded each year, it is important to appreciate that organizations often wipe the OEM build and reload a clean installation that is free from OEM customizations and any third-party software.

You have seen how you can use virtualization software such as Hyper-V to install Windows directly into a virtual environment. Hyper-V can allow you to rapidly provision, modify, save, and even deploy Windows within a fast and efficient tool that is commonly used within organizations.

Microsoft successfully reduces the level of piracy of its software by various methods of activation using product keys. You should know the differences between each key type and the activation methods and be able to choose the most appropriate licensing model for your needs.

Not all installations of Windows result in a clean installation or reinstallation onto new hardware. Often, if a device's hardware is relatively new, it may be suitable to perform an upgrade of the software on the existing hardware. In the next chapter we will explore the various options available to you to upgrade your operating system.

CHAPTER 3

■ ■ ■

Upgrading the Windows Client Operating System

Up until Windows 10, Microsoft historically released several new operating systems per decade. While most PC owners keep the preinstalled version of Windows that came on the system, a large percentage of owners seek to upgrade to the latest version. Most users who upgrade do so to take advantage of the latest functionality that the new system offers. Users who purchase new equipment with the latest operating system can benefit from both additional software functionality and new hardware advancements.

Since Windows Vista, most system hardware has been suitable for upgrading between versions without the need to change processors or increase RAM levels, which means it is easier (and cheaper) for you to upgrade than to purchase a whole new system. The newest devices are often factory sealed, which reduces the option to upgrade hardware components, whereas older systems can still be upgraded with faster hard drives, more RAM, and other components.

Older software can become a serious security risk. Mainstream support for Windows 7 SP1 ended in 2015, and extended support ends on January 14, 2020. It is likely, therefore, that within five years the majority of computers will be running Windows 10. With Windows 10, the free upgrade offer that ran through July 29, 2016, enabled millions of users of Windows 7 Service Pack 1 (SP1) and Windows 8.1 to upgrade directly to Windows 10.

In this chapter, we will review the options and the tools used to upgrade Windows locally and troubleshoot upgrade issues that you may encounter.

Upgrade vs. Clean Installation

Historically, it has generally been better to perform a clean installation whenever possible. This advice is no longer applicable when considering Windows 10, and Microsoft now recommends that you use the upgrade option if you are upgrading from Windows 7SP1 or Windows 8.1 to the latest version of Windows.

© Chris Rhodes and Andrew Bettany 2016
C. Rhodes and A. Bettany, *Windows Installation and Update Troubleshooting*,
DOI 10.1007/978-1-4842-1827-3_3

Clean installations are where you install Windows onto a freshly formatted hard drive. This method is still useful if you have one or more of the following scenarios:

- Installing onto a new hard drive

- Current installation is infected by malware, such as Ransomware, which is difficult to remove

- OEM installation is full of unwanted software, sometimes referred to as bloatware

- Changed system architecture (for example, you added more RAM to your PC, and now want to use an x64 version)

- Using corporate customized image

It is not possible to provide a definitive rule regarding whether your upgrade will be successful. If your operating system has been in use on your computer for more than two years, it may be more appropriate to perform a clean install or reinstatement of the OEM installation, or to restore from one of your early backups or recovery disks. Reinstating the version of Windows that originally came with the device can be useful for several reasons:

- Device drivers should work without any compatibility issues.

- The appropriate system architecture is correctly configured.

- Your device will be activated using the original or OEM-installed version of Windows.

- With a full backup, all installed applications will be restored (although this may also include bloatware).

For organizations that have already created customized images of the desktop, the process of reimaging a device can be performed very quickly and reliably. Typically, the process for building, testing, and finalizing a custom deployment image may take in excess of six months. It may be worth considering testing the upgrade process from your current operating system directly to Windows 10 rather than waiting until a new custom Windows 10 image is available. You may find that this works well, within the earlier adopter or pilot group, as a work around for your system until your deployment team fully evaluates and builds their image.

You can perform an in-place upgrade over the Internet or create standalone installation media and then upgrade offline using the downloaded media. You will see in the following sections that much of the upgrade process and end result is the same, regardless how you instigate the upgrade.

Upgrading and Downgrading Windows

There are only certain upgrade paths available, depending upon which edition of Windows is currently installed. We will focus on the upgrade paths that are available to Windows 7 and Windows 8/8.1 in this chapter. If your system is less than five years old, it should meet the minimum specifications for upgrading to a later version of Windows. You can check whether the device hardware supports Windows 10 by visiting the https://www.microsoft.com/en-us/windows/windows-10-specifications?OCID=win10_null_vanity_win10specs website and reviewing the system requirements listed there.

It is useful to know that even once you have upgraded to Windows 10, you will be able to revert your system back to its original version of Windows.

During the upgrade process, Windows 10 creates a backup of your previous operating system files in the C:\Windows.old folder. After your upgrade to Windows 10, if you are not happy with the new version of Windows, you are able to revert back to the earlier edition. This process is quite painless, and if you revert within 30 days of upgrading, you can navigate to the Recovery section, then the option titled "Go Back to Windows 8.1" within the Settings app, as shown in Figure 3-1.

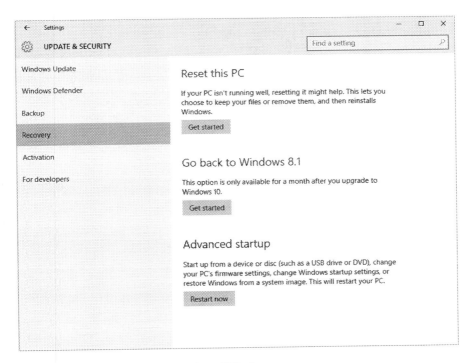

Figure 3-1. *Revert to previous version of Windows*

After 30 days, Windows 10 will automatically delete the previous installed version to release storage space. With the Windows 10, version 1607 (also known as the Anniversary Update), you will only have 10 days to revert to your earlier operating system. On some tablet devices with small hard drives, this is a useful feature. If you need to revert to your previous version after the month has elapsed, you will need to recover from the backup drive that you created prior to the upgrade, or perform a fresh install of your earlier operating system.

If you click the Get Started button for the "Go Back to Windows 8.1" option, you will initiate the process to revert to your earlier operating system. You will be asked to answer a short survey that tells Microsoft why you want to go back. The process will remove any new apps that you have installed and any settings that you have modified since upgrading to Windows 10. Your files should remain after reverting is complete, but it is recommended that you have a backup just in case.

During the reversion process your computer will reboot several times, and it can take some time to complete.

If you want to remove the previous operating system version sooner than the automatic 30 days, you can do so manually by running the Disk Cleanup tool. To run the Disk Cleanup tool follow these steps:

1. Search for Disk Cleanup in the search area.

2. Select the option to "Clean up system files" and allow the Disk Cleanup tool to rescan the drive.

3. Check the "Previous Windows Installation(s)" option (this is not selected by default) as shown in Figure 3-2.

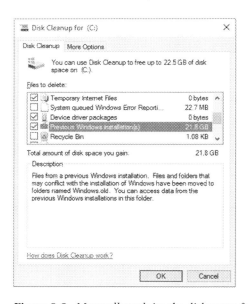

Figure 3-2. *Manually reclaim the disk space from a previous version of Windows*

4. In the Disk Cleanup prompt, "Are you sure you want to permanently delete these files?", select Delete Files.

5. Disk Cleanup will begin file deletion, and the process will provide you with one more warning and confirmation that deleting the previous version of Windows will prevent you from restoring the machine back to the previous version of Windows.

6. Click Yes to confirm. The deletion of the files relating to the previous version of Windows can take several minutes.

There is a built-in Scheduled Task that automatically removes the Windows.old folder after 30 days. On a newly upgraded PC, you can locate the task in Task Scheduler at \Microsoft\Windows\Setup\SetupCleanupTask as shown in Figure 3-3. You may want to edit the scheduled task to run after 60 days or disable the task entirely by removing the enabled check, done within the Triggers tab of the SetupCleanupTask Properties window.

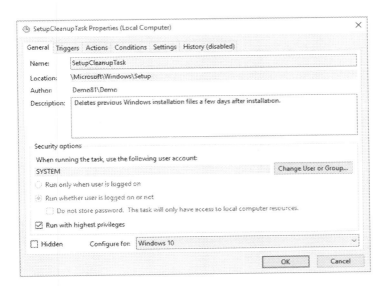

Figure 3-3. Windows.old cleanup of scheduled task

Upgrading the Windows OS from DVD or USB

Although the upgrade is now the recommended deployment method for existing devices running Windows 7 or Windows 8.1 to obtain Windows 10, you can still use other methods, such as "wipe-and-load," using a USB drive or DVD, or over a network if you are deploying a customized corporate image, as you will see in a later chapter.

If you are installing the Windows 10 Home or Pro editions, the easiest way to obtain the Windows 10 installation media is to create your own using the Media Creation Tool (MCT) for Windows 10, as shown in Figure 3-4, which generates a ready-to-use, bootable USB flash drive or an ISO file that you can then burn onto a DVD. The MCT can be downloaded at https://www.microsoft.com/en-gb/software-download/windows10?.

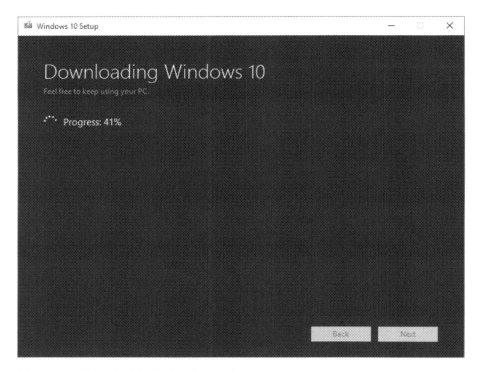

Figure 3-4. *Using the Media Creation Tool*

The MCT tool allows you to specify the language, edition, and architecture (whether x86 or x64, or both) for the installation file and allows you to choose to either save the installation file as an ISO file or copy it directly to a USB flash drive.

When you run the MCT, it will download several gigabytes of files for the installation media, so you should not use this method if you are using a metered or slow Internet connection.

With your Windows DVD or USB now created, you can upgrade the operating system in situ by inserting it into a running Windows 7SP1 or Windows 8.1 machine. If you have downloaded the ISO with the Windows 10 installation media, you can use this to burn it to a DVD or to install Windows 10 into a Hyper-V virtual machine.

To upgrade Windows from installation media you should follow these steps:

1. Insert your Windows 10 media into your computer.

2. Choose "Run Setup.exe" from the popup AutoPlay dialog box.

3. Select Yes from the User Account Control prompt.

4. Windows 10 will install the setup files.

5. If you are connected to the Internet, you should tick the
option to allow setup to Download and Install Updates
(Recommended), as shown in Figure 3-5, as this will ensure
that the latest build of Windows 10 is installed, along with the
latest updates.

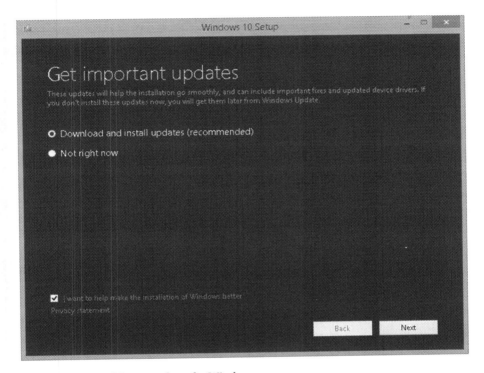

Figure 3-5. *Install latest updates for Windows*

6. Click Next and then click Accept to agree to the license terms.

7. The Setup app checks to see if the device has at least 2 GB of
RAM if you are using x64 architecture as well as sufficient free
disk space for the installation. It will then offer you the option
to change the upgrade options.

8. To review the upgrade options, you should click the "Change
What to Keep" link on the Ready to Install page and make any
changes to the options, as shown in Figure 3-6.

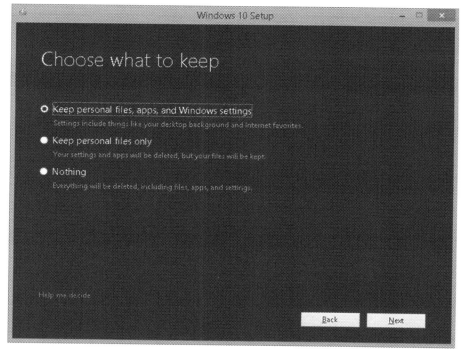

Figure 3-6. *Choose your upgrade options*

9. Click Next and then click Install.

10. Windows 10 Setup will begin the installation phase of the upgrade and may restart during this process.

11. You can cancel the operation at any stage by clicking the Cancel button, as shown in Figure 3-7, and your computer will be returned to its original state.

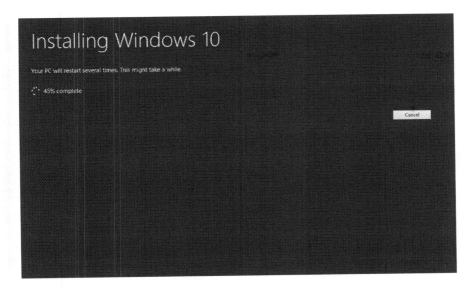

Figure 3-7. You can cancel the upgrade at any time

Once Setup has copied all of the current Windows operating system to the
C:\Windows.old folder, the upgrade will reboot and then continue. You will notice
a change from a blue background to a black screen with a progress indicator, which
provides you with details of the upgrade stages, as shown in Figure 3-8.

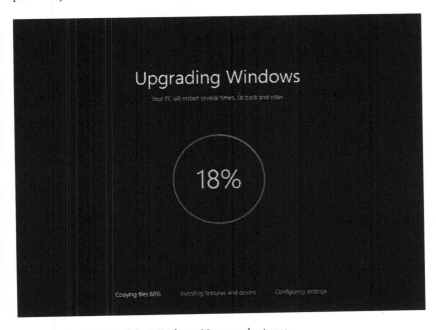

Figure 3-8. Details of the Windows 10 upgrade stages

Upon completion, you will be presented with a "Hi there, welcome back!" screen, as shown in Figure 3-9, which prompts you to verify your login credentials. The system knows who you are, since this is an upgrade, and this prevents an unauthorized user from upgrading your device and gaining access to the system.

Figure 3-9. *Log in to the device during the upgrade to Windows 10*

After you log in to the system you can continue the upgrade process using the steps here:

1. After successful logon you will be offered the Express settings to accept, or you can choose Customize settings.

2. Review the option and click Use Express Settings. (You can modify the settings at any time.)

3. Review the new apps that are built into Windows 10, including Photos, Microsoft Edge, Music, and Movies & TV.

4. Click Next.

5. The upgrade process will reboot a couple more times to complete the upgrade, and then you will be presented with a series of messages that indicate that Windows 10 is setting up your apps.

6. Once the apps have been installed in the background, Windows 10 will display the upgraded desktop, as shown in Figure 3-10.

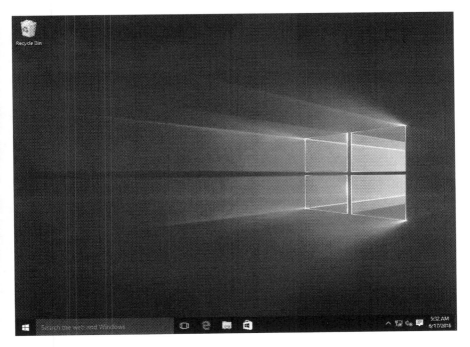

Figure 3-10. *Windows 10 desktop*

Upgrading the Windows OS with Windows Update

One of the painless ways of upgrading Windows is by allowing Microsoft to update your system in a completely automated way. During the first year after release, Windows 10 perfected the upgrade process by rolling out in-place upgrades to millions of home users and Windows Insider program members. Prior to each upgrade, a system recovery point was created, and in the unlikely event that the upgrade was unsuccessful, the system could be easily reverted to the previous state.

Windows 10 will not be issued service packs like previous versions of Windows were. Previous versions received roll-up upgrades as part of a series of service packs, available via Windows Update as follows:

- Windows Vista – Two service packs; last one was available on May 26, 2009

- Windows 7 – Single service pack, available on February 22, 2011

- Windows 7SP1 Convenience roll-up update – available on May 17, 2016 (via the Microsoft Update Catalog website)

- Windows 8 – Upgrade to Windows 8.1 via Windows Update is not available.

- Windows 8.1 – Windows 8.1 Update released on April 8, 2014.

Only certain editions of Windows 7 or 8.1 can be upgraded directly using the Windows Update service, as shown in Table 3-1.

Table 3-1. *Using Windows Update to Upgrade to Windows 10*

SKU to Be Upgraded	Windows Update
Windows 7 Pro	No
Windows 7 Enterprise	No
Windows 7 Pro with SP1	Yes, with update KB 2952664 installed
Windows 7 Enterprise with SP1	No
Windows 8 Pro	No
Windows 8 Enterprise	No
Windows 8.1 Pro	Yes, with updates KB 2919355 and KB 2976978 installed
Windows 8.1 Enterprise	No
Windows 10 Pro (1507)	Yes (if not activated using Key Management Service [KMS])
Windows 10 Enterprise (1507)	Yes (if not activated using KMS)

Businesses with Windows Enterprise editions can upgrade older versions of Windows to the latest offering as part of their enterprise Software Assurance volume licensing benefits.

With the new rapid upgrade cadence now in place to maintain Windows 10, you will see regular upgrading of your system. Microsoft has announced that there will be a minimum of two upgrades to Windows 10 per year. The upgrades are completely separate from the daily, weekly, and monthly security updates that your system also receives.

▓ **Note**   Although Windows RT is now discontinued, you can use the update KB3033055, "Update for Windows RT 8.1 feature improvement," to install the Windows 10–style Start menu on Windows RT devices.

Once you are ready to upgrade, you can use Windows Update to pull down the 2604.5 MB in installation files as an optional update within the Windows Update, which is labeled "Upgrade to Windows 10 Home, Version 1511, 10586," as shown in Figure 3-11.

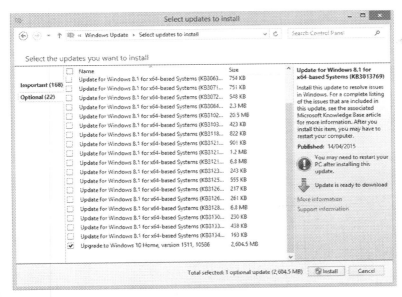

Figure 3-11. *Upgrade to Windows 10 via Windows Update*

If you are familiar with creating installation media, you will have used the Windows image format (WIM) or ISO files before. For the upgrade, Windows 10 uses the new Electronic Software Download (ESD) file format, downloads the image .ESD file to the C:\Windows\SoftwareDistribution\Download folder, and uses the C:\$Windows.~BT\ Sources folder during the actual installation. The ESD file format is a compressed and encrypted version of the .WIM file format and contains just a single Windows image. With the enhanced compression, the ESD file is approximately 30 percent smaller than the .WIM format, which makes it a suitable file format when being delivered through Windows Update.

Once the upgrade has been downloaded, the system will prepare for the upgrade. This includes creating a backup of the system in the Windows.old folder on the system drive. If your computer has low disk space available, the Windows Setup Upgrade Wizard will allow you to store the Windows.old backup folder onto an external drive, such as an external USB drive, thereby freeing up approximately 8 to 10 GB, depending on the version of Windows being upgraded.

Before progressing with the upgrade, you can postpone the actual installation and schedule the upgrade to occur at a more convenient time, such as overnight. At the preferred time, the upgrade will commence automatically.

Once the upgrade process commences, there is no user interaction required, and Windows will automatically restart. An onscreen status indicator will describe the various activities and their progress in the following stages:

- Copying files

- Installing features and drivers

- Configuring settings

Once completed, the upgrade process announces "Welcome to Windows 10!" Here, you will need to enter the password for the user who initiated the in-place upgrade. If the credentials verify against the original Windows installation, the out-of-box-experience (OOBE) sequence commences with the Get Going Fast screen, and Windows 10 introduces new features such as Cortana, as shown in Figure 3-12.

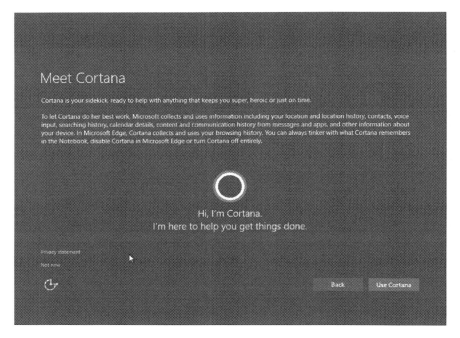

Figure 3-12. *Windows 10 upgrade's Meet Cortana screen*

Once Windows has walked you through the onboarding process, you will be presented with the new Windows 10 desktop, which displays a blue screen with light shining through the Microsoft Windows logo on the right side of the screen.

Upgrading the Windows OS from PC Settings

Once you have upgraded to Windows 10, you can choose whether you want your computer to benefit from the latest upgrades that are made available by Microsoft. Windows 10 will be continuously updated and upgraded by Microsoft, and in theory you should never need to change the operating system again. These upgrades will be referred to as *builds*, and it is expected that Microsoft will release two to four builds each year. By allowing Windows 10 to upgrade, you will see upgrades that allow your system to take advantage when new biometric devices, Trusted Platform Modules (TPM), or processors become available.

If you want early access to the upgraded features, you can join the Windows 10 Insider Preview Program, which is useful so that you can test and evaluate potential upgrades some months before they are released to the mainstream customer base. It is not recommended to use Windows Insider builds in a production environment, but you can use them in a virtual machine or multi-boot scenario.

With the Windows 10 build process, the build will move through progressive branches on its way to the general release and then be made available to enterprise users. A visual representation of how the build and branch development process works is shown in Figure 3-13.

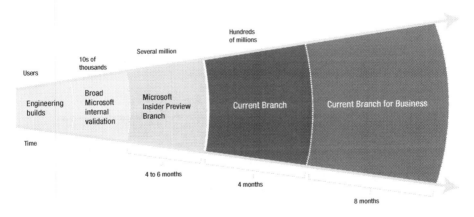

Figure 3-13. *Windows 10 upgrade and build branches timeline*

You should look at the guideline dates along the lower axis, as these roughly define how long each branch will benefit from testing/bug-fixing before the build moves on to the next branch on the right.

You can sign up as a member of the Windows Insider Preview Program by visiting https://insider.windows.com/.

Once you have signed up for Windows Insider, you can decide which of the two levels of adoption of preview builds you want to participate in. The two update speeds are referred to as *rings*:

- Fast ring – You receive the latest build at the earliest opportunity.

- Slow ring – Availability of the build is delayed until it has been exposed to the Fast ring members for a few weeks and the majority of bugs or issues have been addressed.

You can turn off the Insider Preview feature on your computer and revert to the last Current Branch version at any time.

To enable the Insider Preview builds on your Windows 10 computer, follow these steps:

1. Sign up to be part of the Windows Insider Preview Program at https://insider.windows.com/.

2. Sign in to your PC with the Microsoft account you used in Step 1.

3. Open the Settings app.

4. Select Update & Security and then Advanced Options.

5. Click Get Started button under Get Insider Builds section.

6. Read the warning message shown in Figure 3-14 and click Next to continue.

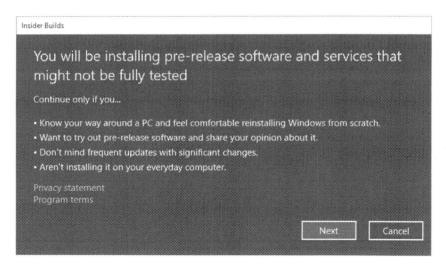

Figure 3-14. *Agreeing to install Windows Insider builds*

7. Restart your PC.

8. Sign back in to your PC with the Microsoft account you used in Step 1.

9. Open the Settings app.

10. Select Update & Security and then Advanced Options.

11. Under Get Insider Builds, you can choose either the Slow or Fast ring.

▓ **Note**   Once you have joined the Windows Insider Preview Program, it can take up to 24 hours before your PC downloads the Fast or Slow ring updates.

Each Current Branch (CB) or Current Branch for Business (CBB) build that is released is assigned a version number that corresponds to the release date, with the year and month in yydd format, such as 1511 or 1607.

The Current Branch for Business servicing option is not available for users running the Home edition of Windows 10. The CBB is meant for enterprises that require extra time for testing and evaluating the build of Windows 10. With the CBB they can defer the upgrade cycle up to one year from each Current Branch release.

If you are a business customer running the Enterprise edition of Windows 10, you can select the "Defer upgrades" option within the Settings app, as shown in Figure 3-15.

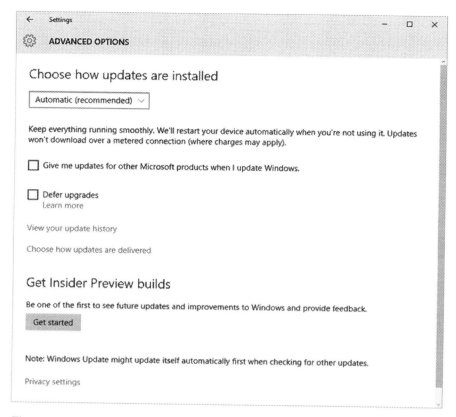

Figure 3-15. *Defer upgrades*

To manually configure your PC to move from the Current Branch to be on the Current Branch for Business, follow these steps:

1. Click the Start button and open Settings screen.

2. Click Update & Security.

3. The Windows Update page opens.

4. Click Advanced Options.

5. Select "Defer upgrades" option.

6. Close Settings screen.

The facility to defer upgrades and join the Current Branch for Business can also be configured using Group Policy, System Center Configuration Manager (SCCM), or the Enterprise Mobility Suite. A new feature–made available with Windows 10, version 1511–called Windows Update for Business allows administrators to further control how upgrades are obtained and allow an additional deferral of upgrades for up to at least eight months.

While deferring upgrades, devices running Windows 10 Pro, Enterprise, and Education on the CBB will continue to receive monthly security updates. When the maximum deferral period has expired, the upgrades will be automatically installed. You will learn about a special build of Windows 10 Enterprise called Long-Term Servicing Branch (LTSB) in Chapter 6.

Troubleshooting Upgrade Issues

Although upgrading to Windows 10 is a great deal more reliable than any other previous Windows upgrade that you may have encountered, there are still potential issues, work-arounds, and best practices that you should be aware of.

You should be wary of systems that may be very old and have previously undergone other upgrades. On most PCs you can often find the original certificate of authenticity (COA) sticker on the chassis of the PC, which will advise you of the OEM-installed version of Windows. If the sticker relates to Windows XP or Vista, you should investigate to see if the internal hardware will support Windows 10. If you have the Get Windows 10 (GWX) app installed, you can check the compatibility report there to make sure your Windows 7 or Windows 8.1 PC can run Windows 10 as follows:

1. Click the Get Windows 10 app icon on the taskbar notification area.

2. Click on the "hamburger" menu button at the top left corner of the app.

3. Click on Check Your PC under the Getting the Upgrade section.

4. Click the "View report" link.

5. Review the compatibility report to see if Windows 10 will work on your system.

You could also check whether the device hardware supports Windows 10 by reviewing the system requirements at https://www.microsoft.com/en-us/windows/windows-10-specifications?OCID=win10_null_vanity_win10specs.

Operating System Stability

If the system you are intending to upgrade is unstable, then it is not a good candidate to upgrade, as you may carry forward any current problems to your new operating system. You should check the reliability of the system by launching the Reliability Monitor. This is done by typing reliability into the Start screen and clicking View Reliability History in the Control Panel. The tool will display a summary of the reliability history for your system, as shown in Figure 3-16.

Figure 3-16. *Reliability Monitor screen*

The Reliability Monitor screen shows a line graph with a scale from 1 to 10 and a date timeline along the bottom axis. The graph rises and falls based on how the system performs. If the system exhibits regular software or driver errors, the system stability may encounter apps crashing or a service stopping. With every system issue that degrades system stability, the graph value will fall, while on a stable system the line graph will rise and be consistently near the maximum level of 10.

The Reliability Monitor is a powerful tool, and you should take a look at your system, using the monitor to drill down into any stability issues that are present.

Troubleshooting Windows 10 Upgrade Error Codes

During the upgrade process, Windows 10 will create an installation log file, which you can inspect to diagnose and troubleshoot what went wrong. The installation log file is located at `C:\windows\Panther\UnattendGC\SetupAct.log`.

As an example, if Windows detects that you are trying to use the wrong installation media, you should find an entry such as "Info [windeploy.exe] OEM license detected, will not run SetupComplete.cmd" within the log file.

Other clues may be found within the `setuperr.log`, which is found at `C:\$Windows.~BT\Sources\Panther\setuperr.log`.

If the problem relates to a compatibility issue, you should review the error code presented. Some of the most common error codes relating to upgrading are shown in Table 3-2.

Table 3-2. Common setuperr.log Upgrade Error Codes

Error Code	Description
0xC1900200	PC does not meet Windows 10 system requirements.
0xC190020E	Insufficient free hard drive space
0xC1900204	Wrong Windows 10 SKU or architecture

Block Upgrading to Windows 10

If you do not want your current system that is running either Windows 7SP1 or Windows 8.1 Update to be upgraded to Windows 10, you can block it by configuring Group Policy settings on your PC as follows:

1. Open Local Group Policy editor by typing gpedit.msc.

2. Expand Computer Configuration.

3. Expand Administrative Templates and then click Windows Components.

4. Expand Windows Update.

5. Double-click "Turn Off the Upgrade to the Latest Version of Windows through Windows Update."

6. Click Enable.

7. Close Local Group Policy editor and reboot your system.

■ **Note** There are several third-party apps that you can install that will prevent your PC from updating to Windows 10, such as Never10, found at https://www.grc.com/never10. htm, or GWX Control Panel, found at http://blog.ultimateoutsider.com/2015/08/ using-gwx-stopper-to-permanently-remove.html.

Once configured, the system will not automatically detect, download, or install the Windows 10 upgrade. You can still upgrade to Windows 10, but you will need to initiate this manually.

Upgrading a System with BitLocker Drive Encryption

If your current system is encrypted using Device Encryption or BitLocker Drive Encryption technology, the Windows 10 upgrade process will automatically process the upgrade, and you won't need to manually disable or suspend the BitLocker. You do not need to decrypt your hard drive prior to upgrading to Windows 10. The upgrade process will recognize that BitLocker is enabled and will suspend the encryption and then resume it after the final configuration reboot. If you don't use a TPM, you will be asked to enter your password or PIN during startup.

If you find that the upgrade process does not recognize the drive as being BitLocker encrypted, you should start the update process using the Setup.exe from within Windows 7SP1 or Windows 8.1 rather than booting directly from the installation media.

It is also a best practice to ensure that you know how to access the BitLocker recovery key in case you forget your password.

Summary

Many experienced users and IT pros may be skeptical about moving away from the traditional wipe-and-load installation process to the newly recommended "in-place upgrade" path. You should review and evaluate the new options available so that you can decide for yourself. Often, the organizations that embrace the latest enhancements in Windows deployment, maintenance, and updating are the ones that benefit from significant savings in both efficiency and costs.

You have seen how you can use the various upgrade methods that are available, such as using Windows Update or the MCT tool, and how to defer upgrades to your enterprise devices using the CBB branch.

You have reviewed several troubleshooting scenarios and learned that not all installations of Windows are suitable for upgrading. In the next chapter, you will explore methods of installing customized builds of Windows using enterprise tools, reference images, and deployment methodologies.

CHAPTER 4

Automating Windows Deployment with Lite Touch

In this chapter, we will be examining the role of Lite Touch in operating systems deployment. Lite Touch describes a methodology for deployment of images to PCs with minimal interaction with the target computer. It all starts with an image.

For many years, systems administrators have sought to achieve what was always seen as the holy grail of desktop deployment: the gold image. So what is a gold image, why seek it, and why is it perhaps almost foolish to embark on such a quest?

It helps to have some historical perspective on this, to see where we are today and how we ended up here. In the days pre-Windows 95 and Window NT 4.0, desktop computers usually came with an Original Equipment Manufacturer (OEM)-installed copy of Windows. Either that, or due to the low count of PCs in networks, they may have gotten their operating system and applications installed manually from CD-ROMs and/or floppy disks. Retrospectively, this has been known as a high-touch deployment. This was not a major pain initially, but as time went on and more and more PCs found their way into companies, automation was sought.

This was not just for the distribution of the operating system, but also for all the "glue" that went with the OS, such as device drivers (which were almost always required to have been manually added to operating systems at that time) and other essential business software, such as anti-virus. New tools started to emerge around the mid-1990s that helped to automate the creation and distribution of operating system images that were crafted by the administrator. Principal among these tools were Ghost and AltIris (although there were others).

So, what is so important about trying to achieve the gold image? Really, it stems from an IT department's desire to have a consistent and supportable environment that allows for ease of reimaging if a computer runs into problems. This makes it uneconomic to spend excessive amounts of time in troubleshooting and fixing the computer, compared to the time and energy expended in reimaging with the gold image.

© Chris Rhodes and Andrew Bettany 2016
C. Rhodes and A. Bettany, *Windows Installation and Update Troubleshooting*,
DOI 10.1007/978-1-4842-1827-3_4

> ▧ **Note**   Lite touch is not only a concept, but also describes the process and the set of tools that are used to achieve this. In today's environments, this is usually done using the Microsoft Deployment Toolkit (MDT), Windows Deployment Services (WDS), and some manual steps performed by an engineer at the PC itself. By its very definition, in lite touch the support engineer is physically touching the PC, albeit in a limited way, and is not expected to press every button and check every checkbox that an installation would otherwise require. Lite touch differs from zero-touch deployments in that zero touch does not require any physical presence at the PC to undertake a deployment. This is achieved by using management tools such as Microsoft Systems Center Configuration Manager (SCCM).

Creating a Reference Machine (Sysprep)

So, let's imagine that you have decided that creating an image is the way to go to deploy a new operating system version to your computers (as opposed to in-place upgrades). What should go in your image? Should you keep it skinny and have a minimal number of applications and other software installed in it, or should you install every variation of software so that everyone is catered for? In reality, this is not possible due to licencing implications. You don't need to install every application into your image however, for it to be described as a thick image. While it is impractical to install them all, there is a case for installing a majority of applications into an image for ease of use once the image arrives at the PC.

These extremes are known as thin and thick images, respectively. In each case, whether you decide to go thin, thick, or something in between, you need to start off by having a reference computer to work on.

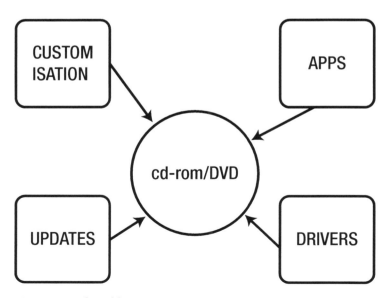

Figure 4-1. *The gold image*

▨ **Note** Thin images are not simply left thin. They are augmented post-deployment with applications and other required components, such as printers. This augmentation is performed with a variety of tools, such as SCCM, Group Policies, App-V, and RemoteApp. In the case of App-V and RemoteApp, the applications are not even installed on the PC, meaning a very agile deployment with few dependencies.

The reference computer could be a physical machine, which would be meaningful if it represented the majority of the installed bases of hardware in the environment, or it could be a virtual machine. Having a virtual machine makes a lot of sense. It's hardware independent, has no requirements for extra device drivers, and is extremely portable–another tech support person could import it to their computer and work on it equally the same. This also means that any bloat from manufacturer drivers or third-party packaged applications that may come with a new PC is minimized.

Any potential issues with hardware are also kept to a minimum with a virtual machine, especially if using Hyper-V to host it, as Windows operating systems today do not require any drivers or customization to allow them to recognize the fact they are running on a hypervisor; they can be said to be driver-neutral. Another advantage is that you can utilize Hyper-V checkpoints for testing, which can reduce the time between test iterations. This is typically the way that reference computers are created today.

One thing to bear in mind is that, ultimately, images (built from the reference computer) are only relevant to the environment in which they are created and must include all the components relevant to that environment. So what should you include in the image? As Figure 4-1 shows, you should think about a line of business applications, device drivers, Windows updates, and any other customization that is relevant to the business of applications or the operating system environment. This, then, is your SOE, or standard operating system environment, but it is not yet an image.

You can either build a reference image manually or use automation, such as utilising MDT. As we will be examining MDT in more detail later, let's look at how to build it manually for now. This may be regarded as a high-touch method, but it is intended to only have to be done once anyway.

One possible way to build a reference image is to take a retail DVD media disc and construct an answer file using Windows System Image Manager (SIM) (see later in this chapter for more information). The answer file contains the answers that the setup program questions during setup, such as which drive to install to and which language/regional settings to use.

A simple walkthrough on how to build the reference computer on a physical computer is as follows:

1. Create an answer file using Windows SIM.

2. Place answer file on the root of a USB drive and insert it into the computer.

3. Run Setup from the DVD media.

4. Configure Windows settings.

5. Install updates.

6. Install applications and configure them.

Alternatively, skip Steps 1 and 2 and run setup manually from the installation media. This route is convenient when building a virtual machine–based reference computer and installing Windows from an ISO file.

Once Windows is installed, it's time to configure any aspects of the operating system that the business requires, such as applying any initial first-run configuration steps. Applications that are considered core, like Microsoft Office, may get installed at this time if it makes sense to include it, versus installation post-deployment using another mechanism like SCCM.

One challenge administrators traditionally face is ensuring that the image that eventually gets created doesn't go "stale" too quickly. You could install all the relevant updates to Windows at the time of building the reference computer, but over time more updates will inevitably be released by Microsoft. This would mean that the reference computer would get progressively more out of date and require time to get the deployed operating system updated and ready for use by the end user. The time taken to install a back catalog of updates can be longer than it took to deploy the image, thus being somewhat self-defeating.

▨ **Tip** Once the reference computer is saved as an image, it's important to have a strategy for keeping the image up to date. This used to involve deploying the image, updating it, preparing it for capture once more, and then recapturing it. Now, it is possible to add updates to offline images using DISM. An example of this is seen here:

```
Dism /Add-Package /PackagePath:/PackagePath:C:\MSU\Windows10-KB12345678-x64.
msu /Image:C:\mount\boot /LogPath:AddPackage.log
```

This is only an excerpt of the steps required. More information can be found at

https://msdn.microsoft.com/en-us/windows/hardware/commercialize/manufacture/
desktop/add-updates-to-customized-windows-and-winpe-images

Now that that reference computer is built and includes the components that we wanted, we can start to think about creating an image of this computer, with the intention of cloning it to dozens of other computers. However, it's not possible just to "just clone it." Some work needs to be done to remove any specifics, such as the computer name and other settings, that would be incompatible with cloning. This process is known as *generalizing*.

To generalize a computer, you must run the system preparation tool sysprep.exe in the generalize mode. Generalizing a computer prepares it for imaging by removing system restore points, clearing event logs, and removing the computer name, among other tasks.

▨ **Tip** You must use the version of Sysprep that is provided with the Windows version that you intend to configure. Sysprep is included in every installation of Windows and can be found in %WINDIR%\system32\sysprep.

Figure 4-2 shows Sysprep in action. There are two cleanup actions that can be specified. The main one that prepares a system for imaging is the *Enter System Out-Of-Box Experience (OOBE)* mode. This mode, upon the rebooting of the computer, would put the computer into the `specialize` pass of Windows Setup, requiring information like a computer name and a user name to be entered to finish off the installation. An answer file for this stage can be created using Windows SIM and will be explained later.

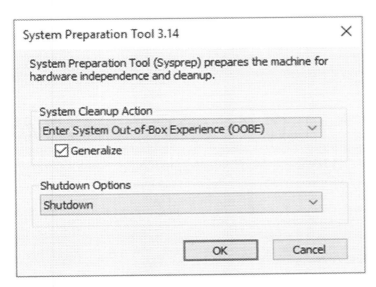

Figure 4-2. *The System Preparation Tool (Sysprep.exe)*

The other mode is *Enter System Audit* mode, which puts the computer into audit mode after the next reboot. Audit mode allows for engineers to test configurations before committing to a signed-off build for imaging. Think of it almost like a try-before-you-buy mode that would be used prior to generalizing. This allows for a complete bypass of the OOBE pass and access to the desktop for validation of the reference computer, or any other last minute additions, such as drivers.

Chapter 1 contains information on running Sysprep from a command line and the syntax to be used, which also allows for a custom answer file to be used.

It's worth noting that there is a limit to how many times Sysprep can be run against an activated system, which is three for older versions such as Windows Vista and Windows 7, while for Windows 8.1 and Windows 10 it's eight times. Technically, Sysprep itself can be run an unlimited number of times, but the activation clock of the computer starts once it has been activated the first time. A workaround to this is using virtual machines, specifically checkpoints, as recommended earlier. A better way to avoid this limit is to add a specific product key into an answer file in the `Microsoft-Windows-Shell-Setup\ProductKey` section of the `specialize` pass. This will kick up the need to activate again on the deployed computer.

■ **Note** There is a widely perceived notion that running Sysprep is essential in order to avoid having computers with duplicate security identifiers or SIDs. SIDs are generated on each computer during Windows Setup and form the basis of the ID for accounts on that computer. For many years, administrators thought that generalizing a computer was essential to avoiding duplicate SIDs. In reality, this is a myth, as it makes no practical day-to-day difference on a client computer.

The shutdown options also include reboot and quit. Normally, shutdown is used, as it allows you to take your time getting ready to start the machine up for capturing it with bootable media (WinPE).

Creating Unattended Installations (Windows SIM)

Moving from high touch to lite touch is where automation begins to take hold. To this end, you will need to start looking at creating answer files that will provide the input that Windows Setup would normally expect to be passed in using end-user manual input, such as typing the computer name.

One of the tools in the Windows ADK that will be required for this is Windows Setup Image Manager (Windows SIM). Windows SIM is designed to help administrators tailor their own answer files to be used in the following common scenarios:

- For building a reference computer from media

- For building a regular computer from media

- To accompany sysprep.exe to help finalize post-imaging setup (OOBE)

The answer files that Windows SIM will help create are XML based and could really be edited in a text editor if you had the will to do so. In reality, this is too time consuming, and an intimate knowledge of all of the settings available in the different passes of Windows Setup would be required. Windows SIM exposes these settings for us, so no guesswork is required. The first step in using SIM is to add an existing image in the Windows Image section. A good place to start (as you haven't created a custom image yet) is to use install.wim from a Windows ISO or DVD. This is the shipped copy of Windows that a normal computer is installed from. It's a good idea to copy all of the source files to your hard drive first so there are no issues relating to read-only media. Typically, you need to catalog this so that the tool enumerates the configurable settings and packages from inside the image. Once this is done, you will create a new answer file in the middle pane.

Next, you will expand the Components and Packages area in the image and view the components that you wish to add to your answer file to customize Windows Setup. Settings may be applied to one or more than one pass, depending on the relevance of the settings in it. The available choices are displayed once you click on a component, as shown in Figure 4-3.

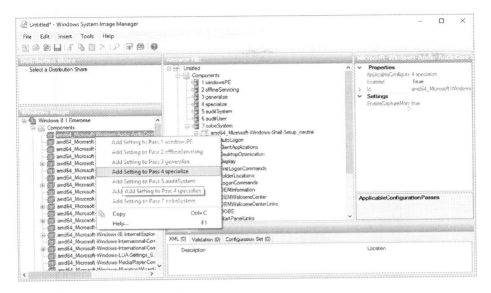

Figure 4-3. *Windows SIM interface*

You may recall from Chapter 1 that there are seven passes (phases) of Windows Setup, which are:

windowsPE

offlineServicing

generalize

specialize

auditSystem

auditUser

oobeSystem

These passes control the processing of the Windows Setup process, and there are defined tasks that occur at these different stages. That said, some tasks can be performed in more than one pass.

Once a component has been added to the relevant pass of Setup, you can start to customize the data using the middle and right-hand panes in the tool. For example, in Figure 4-4, Windows Mail has been configured to be hidden.

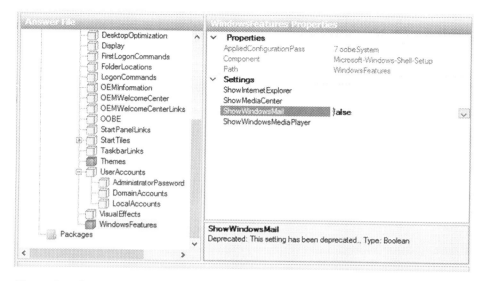

Figure 4-4. *Customizing components in Windows SIM*

If making an answer file for automated installation from a media-based install (as described in the section earlier relating to building a reference computer), you would save the file as autounattend.xml. This is what the Windows Setup program is hard coded to look for on removable media drives, such as a USB drive, during the first stage of setup. If located, it automatically uses it and processes it.

Packages can be added to the answer file in addition to the settings from components just discussed. Packages include updates and language packs. Packages can be added or removed from the image. The concept of removing packages includes the ability to remove some in-box software from users that may not be desirable in a corporate environment, such as Windows Media Player. Packages are configured only in the offlineServicing pass. This is similar to how DISM was mentioned before for adding Windows updates to offline images to keep them fresh.

▓ **Note** Answer files can be called anything (except the autounattend.xml file used for media-based installs in conjunction with a USB drive). However, it is common practice to name the setup answer file Unattend.xml. You would then use the answer file by calling it as a parameter of Windows Setup; for example:

```
Setup.exe /unattend:unattend.xml
```

If you were creating an answer file to automate a sysprepped computer coming into the OOBE stage after deploying an image, your syntax going into Sysprep may look something like this:

```
Sysprep /generalize /oobe /unattend:C:\unattend.xml /shutdown
```

Once you've edited the answer file, it is a great idea to have it validated before saving it and using it. Validation checks that the entered values are relevant to the data type expected. This does not mean that your answer file is 100 percent guaranteed to work, but it will eliminate common typos and mistakes. Testing is really the only way to tell for sure that it works!

■ **Note**   There are so many settings that can be customized that it's a good idea to use the in-built documentation inside Windows SIM to help answer any questions you may have regarding what the settings do and what values you can assign to them. There are too many to list in this book.

Configure and Troubleshoot WDS

Now that you have created a reference computer and run Sysprep on it, the next task is to copy that computer into an image. You could do that locally, using DISM to create a WIM file that contains your image.

Figure 4-5 shows an example of how that might look.

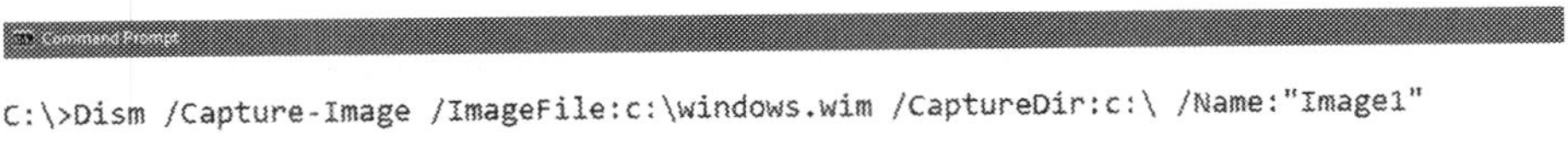

```
Command Prompt
C:\>Dism /Capture-Image /ImageFile:c:\windows.wim /CaptureDir:c:\ /Name:"Image1"
```

Figure 4-5. *Capturing an image with DISM*

This command would capture the contents of the C: drive into a file named c:\ windows.wim and associate a name of image1 with the stored image. (You may recall we discussed the WIM file format in Chapter 1.) This needs to be run from outside of Windows itself. Following the line of logic in this chapter, we would by now have run Sysprep and shut down the computer. To get to this point of capturing a reference computer, you will need to boot into an operating system that allows for the capture to take place, but does not interfere with Sysprep and the OOBE pass that will follow.

This is called WinPE (Windows Preinstallation Environment). WinPE (or a custom version of it) is what is used during Windows Setup. The Windows ADK provides tools to create your own WinPE media, which can be used to boot from a USB drive, for example. A run-through of how to create this is found in Chapter 1. Once booted into this cut-down version of Windows, a limited set of tools are made available, but all that is needed here is a basic command line to perform the capture using DISM.exe.

▪ **Note**   WIM files are not images. WIM files can contain one or more images. Multiple images can be stored within the same file. This results in storage efficiency, as files are single-instanced. In other words, if you were creating three images based on Windows 10, the duplication of files would be avoided, and the size of the WIM containing the images would be less than the sum of its parts. Add to that the fact that you can also compress files in a WIM and you get highly effective storage for your images.

Installing a WDS Server

This is useful to know; however, on a large corporate network this is a little clunky, especially when considering you may need to deploy that image hundreds of times over. There is an alternative, and that is to use Windows Deployment Services (WDS). WDS acts as a repository for WIM images on the network, with many added advantages.

WDS has the capability to serve images to clients over the network using PXE boot. PXE boot is a special function of network interface cards that supports booting the computer to the network rather than booting from a hard drive. This requires no operating system to be present on the computer, as the network stack required is included in the PXE specification. Clients boot to the network, acquire an IP address from DHCP, and then locate the WDS server automatically.

Sound good? Let's install WDS and look at how to create and distribute images using the network rather than DISM and WinPE locally. In Windows Server 2012 R2 and above, WDS is an installable role. When you install it, there are two role services, as shown in Figure 4-6. Installing both of these on the same server is the typical configuration.

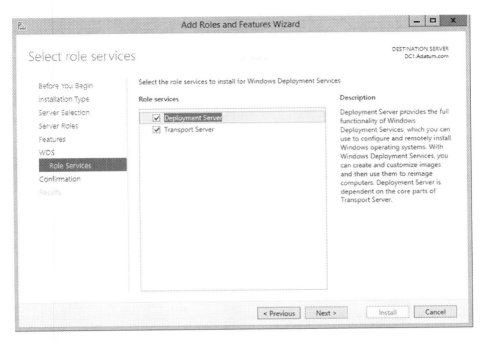

Figure 4-6. *Installing WDS*

Once WDS is installed, it requires configuration to have it be ready for use on the network. The following settings need to be configured as part of the post-installation wizard:

- There is a choice whether to install WDS as a standalone service on the network or to integrate with Active Directory (AD). Generally, it is integrated with Active Directory so that you can work with OU containers for the storage of computer accounts, (which would need to be created anyway once a computer joins a domain) and to leverage AD groups for assignment of permissions on images to restrict access. You may install it standalone if you are working on a client site and using your own server to distribute images as a one-off rather than the customer's server.

- Path to store image files. This is straightforward. Tell the wizard where you would like to store images. It defaults to `C:\RemoteInstall`, but usually WDS servers have other disks provisioned for this purpose because of capacity and performance reasons.

- Should the server respond to clients? While you can have it live by default, in practice it makes sense to say no initially then activate it later once you actually have some images ready to upload or capture.

- DHCP options. WDS listens on port 67, like DHCP servers do
  for lease generation for IP addresses. There can be a conflict,
  however, if the DHCP server is the same server as the WDS server.
  The wizard looks to remedy this if it detects this scenario. More
  information about this, and different related scenarios, will be
  covered later in the last section of this chapter.

Once configured, the WDS administration console looks like the one in Figure 4-7.

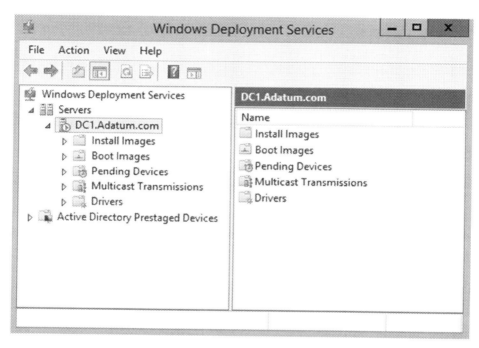

Figure 4-7. *The WDS console*

Getting to Know WDS

Within the Servers container, each WDS server added has a number of default containers.
Install Images is where your WIM-based images will logically reside (wherever
they may rest on the hard drive). Images can be stored in image groups for ease of
administration. Boot Images is where your WinPE images will live. These can be created
using the Windows ADK and added here, or built using standard ones from the Windows
Setup ISOs/DVDs (more on this shortly).

Pending Devices is a container to use if you have decided to set the PXE response
setting in the wizard to require admin approval. This means that each unknown client
that requests to connect to the WDS server must be manually approved before an image
can be distributed. If the server is using automatic approval for clients, then this container

is redundant. This setting is configurable using the properties on the server, as shown in Figure 4-8. The setting recommended in the wizard would be the first option, but you then change it once ready to receive clients. "Known clients" refers to computers that are prestaged in AD. More about prestaging will be covered later.

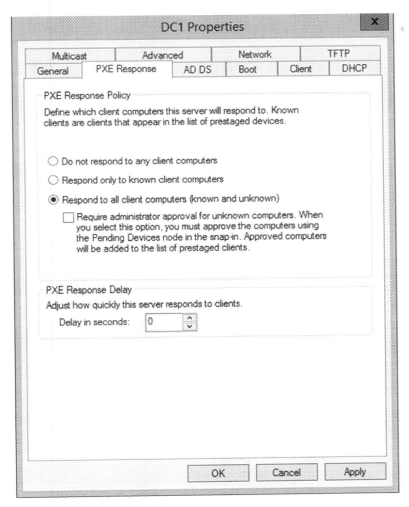

Figure 4-8. *Configuring the PXE response settings*

The Multicast Transmissions container is where an administrator can create a multicast job that will be deployed to a number of client computers simultaneously using a multicast stream (as opposed to clients' receiving an image using 1:1 unicast transmissions). This is very useful when deploying the same image to a room full of computers at the same time. The image is preselected, and either the stream begins when

101

a specified threshold number of computers is reached or auto-cast is used to continue deploying the image until all computers have received it, even if they did not start at the same time as the other computers.

Finally, the Drivers container is where device driver packages can be grouped together and added to images, which will be covered later.

Boot Images

So, now the server is built, the next task is to add images. Let's start with the boot images. There are two choices here. You can either upload into the console WinPE images that you already made using the ADK tools (as long as they are in WIM format), or you can import a WIM from a Windows Setup disc or ISO file.

▓ **Tip** If you view a Windows Setup ISO or DVD, you will find a folder called \Sources. This contains two WIM files, Boot.wim and Install.wim. Install.wim contains the install image(s) that a normal setup of Windows would use. Boot.wim contains a WinPE-based image, which is what Windows Setup uses for the installation process. You can add either or both of these as starters to help you get up and running quickly in WDS.

If you decide to use a boot.wim file from an ISO, you will need to convert this after adding it into two further images, a capture and a discover image. The capture image is used when a PXE client is started up, with the intention of capturing a reference computer. A discover image is used for PXE clients when they want to download an image from WDS. Each image is broadly the same, but has different user interface options for each use case.

▓ **Note** You should consider a mixed environment where there are 32-bit and 64-bit client computers. You can either standardize having only 32-bit discover and capture images, or have iterations of both. Due to the CPU architecture, 32-bit computers cannot use 64-bit images, but 64-bit computers can use either type of image.

Install Images

Once the boot images are added, you may need to add drivers to them to account for device driver requirements for the WinPE stage of setup. Primarily, this would be network card drivers and disk controller drivers to allow for setup to complete. All other drivers should be added to the install image, such as video card drivers. Note that this may also involve duplicating the drivers added to the boot images too, as these are only relevant to the PE phase, are used only during that time from RAM, and are not persistent on the target computers.

Just like the boot images, install images need to be added. Install images can be sourced from the following:

- A standard `install.wim` file from a Windows disc/ISO

- a WIM you have previously created offline

- a new capture from a reference computer

Again, an easy way to get started is to add an image like Windows 10 Enterprise from an ISO using the "Add Install Image" option on the `Install Images` container.

Once an install image is added, some options can be configured on the image, such as permissions for who is allowed to install it (otherwise, anyone might be able to PXE boot any computer and receive a corporate image from WDS). You can also associate an answer file with the image that you have previously authored in Windows SIM, as shown in Figure 4-9.

Figure 4-9. Adding an answer file to an image in WDS

To test that WDS is working, take a computer with PXE support (a virtual machine is best, as it has native support for this without any other drivers, and can easily be reset after testing) and attempt to boot to the network. For most computers, F12 on the keyboard (or Enter, for virtual machines) must be pressed to confirm the network boot. Once the client computer has found the WDS server and acquired its IP address, a menu is shown, such as the one seen in Figure 4-10.

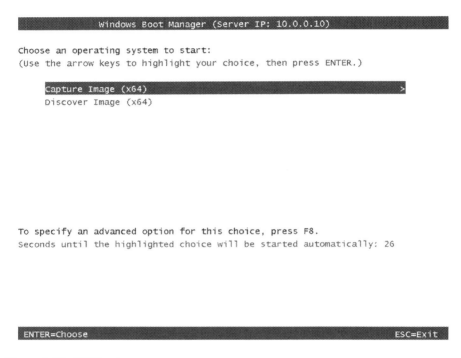

Figure 4-10. PXE boot menu

Here, you can see the capture and discover images that you created earlier. You can now image a machine that was prepared with Sysprep up to the server, or download one to the computer.

▓ **Tip**   Naming your images with an easy-to-understand naming convention, such as the one in Figure 4-10, will help your technicians connect correctly to WDS.

Troubleshooting WDS

There are many moving parts to WDS, as it relies on several server-side components, as well as on PXE and the network, to all behave in order for it to work. In this section, we will look at some of the main areas that can go wrong and how to remedy them.

One of the most common issues that arises is having the incorrect DHCP settings, such as missing options or incorrect server names or boot file names.

Scenario	DHCP Configuration
WDS and DHCP running on the same server	WDS must not listen on port 67. Set this during the configuration wizard or later using the DHCP properties tab on the server in the WDS console, as shown in Figure 4-11. Ensure you set both checkboxes as advised. Usually done if DHCP is detected as being installed first. Ensure that option 60 is set in the DHCP scope/server options with a value of PXEClient.
WDS and DHCP running on different servers in the same subnet	No configuration needed on WDS or DHCP. Broadcasts allow clients to find both servers, which listen on port 67–DHCP for the IP address allocation and WDS for requests to find it (both share the same port).
WDS and DHCP running on different servers in different subnets	Configure options 66 and 67 in DHCP scope options. Ensure that option 66 details the WDS server name and 67 has the boot file name of either boot\x86\pxeboot.com or boot\x64\pxeboot.com for 32-bit and 64-bit client support, respectively.

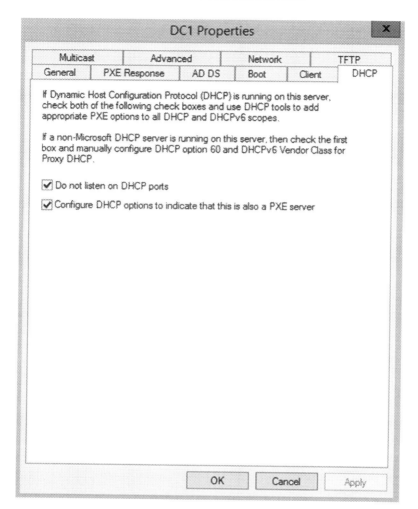

Figure 4-11. *DHCP settings*

Permissions on images can be a problem. The user performing the installation needs NTFS permissions that allow them to read the relevant image file(s). Check group memberships and the access control lists to ensure they can read them. Usually, default permissions are fine, but it's something to check that would prevent access to deploying an image.

Reference computers will fail to capture unless they have had Sysprep applied first. This is actually checked by the capture image process, and capturing is halted if it is not found.

Clients' not booting to the network correctly is a common problem. Not all computers may have the capability to perform PXE boots. Verify the network card can perform this, and also check the PXE boot option in the computer's BIOS or UEFI, and that the boot order has PXE at the top of the boot priority list.

Not having the right architecture boot images (x86/x64) is something to check as well. x64 clients can happily use x86 boot images and x64 images, but x86 clients can only use their own architecture images and will fail to locate boot images when PXE booting. You can check which are available in the Boot Images container in the WDS console.

Configure and Troubleshoot MDT

Microsoft Deployment Toolkit, or MDT, is a free download tool from Microsoft that takes deployment to another level, one of greater automation. MDT is not part of the Windows ADK, so you must remember to download it separately (it's approximately 20 MB in size). You can download the Microsoft Deployment Toolkit from https://technet.microsoft.com/windows/dn475741.aspx.

▓ **Tip** Always download the latest version of MDT, as it is constantly being revised for new scenarios and operating systems. At the time of going to print, the current version is 2013 Update 2. Ensure that the Windows ADK is installed before installing MDT. The versions of MDT are tied to the ADK versions.

So, why do I need MDT in my life if I already have WDS and Windows SIM and the other components of the Windows ADK? MDT can also be integrated with WDS and SCCM (which will be covered in the next chapter). MDT is designed to help create end to end solutions for deployment in order to create the lightest lite-touch process possible without going the whole hog and using SCCM for zero-touch installations.

MDT has a management tool interface called the Deployment Workbench that contains two main nodes: Information Center (documentation of how it works) and Deployment Shares (the bit you configure). The first thing you must do with MDT is to create a Deployment Share, which can be located on the local computer. The Deployment Share is a shared folder that contains all the components that you will use for deployments, such as scripts, driver packages, and images.

Once a share is provisioned, the full structure of MDT can be properly seen, as shown in Figure 4-12. You will recognize some similarities to WDS here, such as drivers, but also some new containers, like applications.

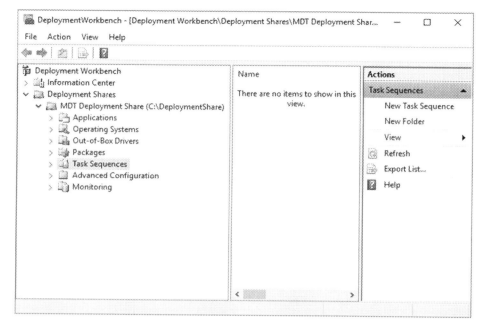

Figure 4-12. *Deployment Workbench*

Task Sequences

Essentially, with MDT you will create task sequences, which are deployment processes that incorporate installing the operating system, drivers, applications, and more to client computers.

There are several key task sequences that you can leverage that MDT has precreated the structure of. These are shown in Figure 4-13. This includes scenarios like building the reference computer in the first place or new installations or upgrades of Windows. A good place to start is the Standard Client Task Sequence. This walks you through the process of installing Windows with automation.

New Task Sequence Wizard

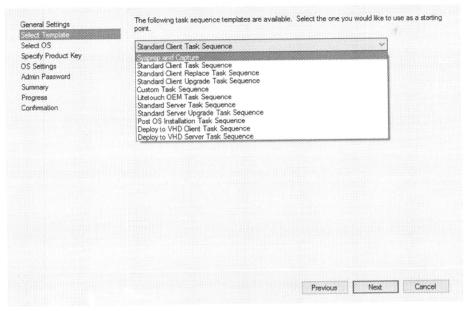

Figure 4-13. *The New Task Sequence Wizard*

■ **Note**   Before building task sequences, you need to populate MDT with the building blocks that MDT uses, such as operating systems, drivers, applications, and language packs.

As we need at least an operating system for this task sequence, we will look at adding that first and come back to the task sequence later. Adding an operating system gives you the choice of adding one of the following:

- A full set of source files (such as from an ISO)

- Custom image file (from a WIM you previously built)

- An image stored on WDS (that you previously created)

Now that the Deployment Share contains at least an operating system, we can create the task sequence. Start the task sequence by configuring the general settings for information such as name and ID. Then, after selecting the sequence type from the templates just mentioned, you can pick from operating systems you have previously added, as shown in Figure 4-14.

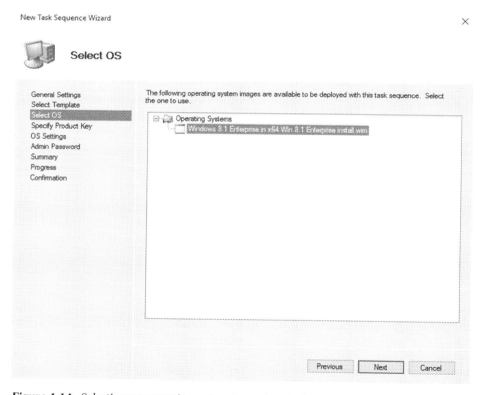

Figure 4-14. *Selecting an operating system image in a task sequence*

Information can be added to the operating system–similar to with answer-file creation in Windows SIM–such as product key and admin password. Remember, of course, that the ADK components live underneath MDT, so we are building on the tools already installed and adding interfaces to those tools here. Of course, for true lite touch, you need to automate as much as possible, but anything left blank that setup would require will result in a user prompt during setup. The goal usually is to streamline this so that once the task sequence is in motion on a client computer the technician can walk away and leave it.

After the task sequence is created, you will need to go back and edit some of the settings to suit your requirements; for example, adding applications or partitioning the hard drive before installation. An example of this is shown in Figure 4-15, where an application is added to the sequence.

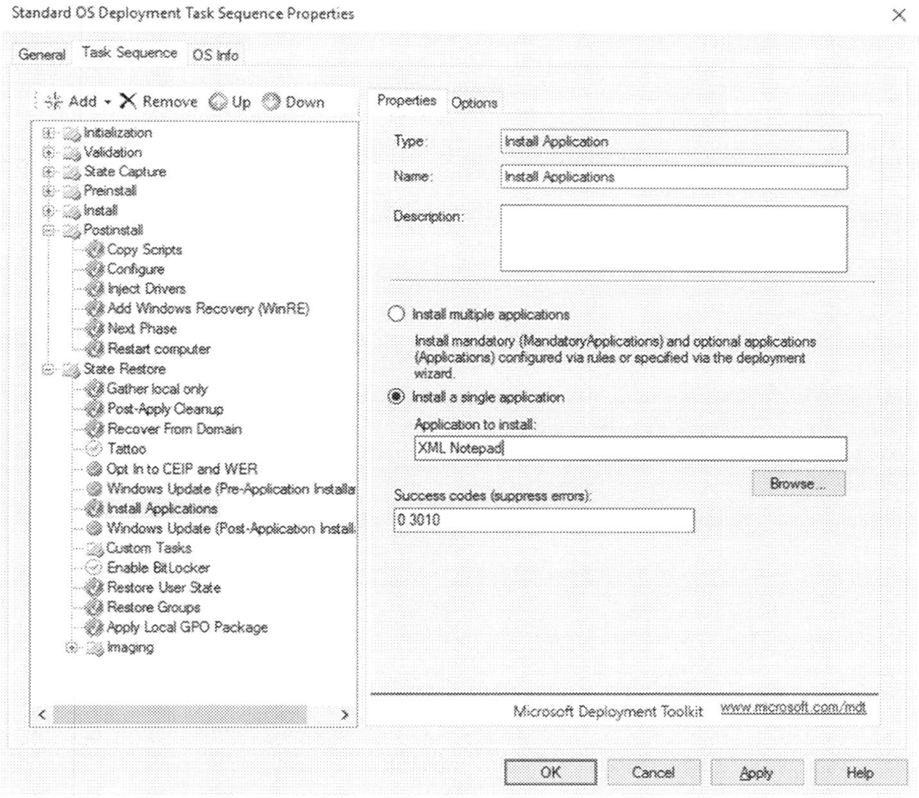

Figure 4-15. *Editing a task sequence*

111

Adding Applications

Application source files can be added to the Deployment Share for integration into your task sequences. More complex task sequences will add applications to the deployed operating system as a post-installation process (as opposed to them being included in the image in the first place). While you can potentially add any application, you need to make sure that the application can be installed without user intervention. For example, you could install a Windows Installer–based application by specifying the /q parameter on the command line when running the setup program, such as XMLnotepad.msi /q.

▓ **Tip** Testing is generally important for task sequences anyway, but especially for application installers that you want to run silently (without user intervention). It may take a few runs before you get it to run perfectly, as you may need to supply information in an XML or other file for input to the installation program.

To add an application to the Deployment Share, in the workbench, right click Applications and add the application, pointing the wizard to where the installation files reside so that they can be added to the share or referenced from a network share. It's common practice for administrators to manage a software share on the network for centrally locating application installation programs. This can also include scripts and transform files used for silent installation and is useful in helping keep software up to date without having to rebuild the whole image.

Packages

One useful feature of MDT is the ability to add other OS packages to the task sequence. For example, this can include language packs, Windows update packages, and other related files. These must be in the file format of .CAB or .MSU for installation to the image. Adding packages is done similarly to how applications are added–by pointing the wizard to the source files' folder on the drive, which adds them to the Deployment Share.

Updating the Deployment Share

Once you have created a task sequence or configured any settings in MDT, you will be required to update the Deployment Share. This step is not obvious to the uninitiated, but is essential. This process checks for changes and rebuilds a boot image incorporating the new changes made. This boot image is created as both a WIM file and an ISO file. You can then choose to add this to WDS as a boot image or add it to a USB drive for booting without WDS. It is possible to build USB media that contains everything that is needed to provision a remote computer without the network being present, which is ideal for remote workers, such as field engineers or home workers. Again, ADK is being used underneath to full effect to build the media.

To test the media, you can either boot using the lite-touch boot image from USB or WDS or connect to the Deployment Share and run the script to load the Deployment Wizard, which controls the rest of the process on the client computer (such as `\\server\DeploymentShare$\Scripts\LiteTouch.vbs`).

Troubleshooting MDT

MDT itself is pretty complex, but also builds upon many other components, so troubleshooting can be tricky. Add to that the fact that most clients are connecting over a network to the Deployment Share and/or WDS and you almost have a recipe for disaster! Well, maybe not quite that bad, but you need a sound methodology for approaching troubleshooting. Try to understand what's going wrong and why. For instance, if you cannot update the Deployment Share, do you have access to the share? Are the WinPE components from ADK installed?

■ **Tip** Ensure all relevant ADK components installed; otherwise, updating Deployment Share can fail—for example, if you did not have the WinPE components installed. You will need at least Deployment Tools, WinPE, and optionally USMT tools and ICD from the ADK.

Sometimes the easy things are the ones that are overlooked, so it's well worth checking access control lists for the share and NTFS permissions for the accounts performing lite-touch deployments on the Deployment Share. Note also that by default the share is a hidden share (it ends with a $; for example, `deploymentshare$`) so don't expect to easily browse to it over the network!

From a diagnostics perspective, we are well catered for with MDT—it's almost like they expect it to fail! On a client performing a lite-touch installation, a series of logs are created that can be interpreted if there is a failure. These live in `C:\MININT\SMSOSD\OSDLOGS` during setup and later get moved to `%WINDIR%\SMSOSD` or `%WINDIR%\TEMP\SMSOSD` after a successful installation.

Among the logs is `BDD.log`, which is the main aggregated log to check. There are also other logs, such as `LiteTouch.log` and `WPEinit.log`, that cover specific stages of lite touch in more detail. The logs require a tool called Trace32 to help read them, which is freely available online as part of the SCCM 2007 Toolkit. For more information, see `https://technet.microsoft.com/en-us/library/dn781088.aspx`.

One area of MDT that has a massive amount of potential is two rule files named `customsettings.ini` and `bootstrap.ini`. While they are fairly simple in construction, the breadth of settings that these can touch during a lite-touch install are vast. It can vary from whether to join a domain to more complex operations. You can edit the files directly, but it's easier to access them from the Rules tab and the Windows PE tab, respectively, within the Deployment Share properties screen.

An example of a `bootstrap.ini` file is shown next. The bootstrap file is copied to the WinPE media, which is another reason why you need to update the Deployment Share when you make a change:

```
[Settings]
Priority=Default
[Default]
DeployRoot=\\server\DeploymentShare$
UserDomain=Adatum
UserID=Technician1
UserPassword=Pa$$w0rd
SkipBDDWelcome=Yes
```

`Customsettings.ini` follows the same `.ini` file structure as just seen, but contains settings such as time zone, domain join settings, admin password, and other OOBE settings. It goes without saying that although it provides for great customization, it is only a text file, so it is prone to user error in the form of typos and malformed parameters and values.

Deployment Hints, Tips, and Shortcuts (Including Activation Issues)

As you have picked up on while reading this chapter, there are lots of technical tools, files, and settings that make up a successful lite-touch deployment. Understanding these moving parts is key to ensuring deployment success. From experience over the years, there are a few tips to pass on that will help ensure that your deployments run smoothly.

Activation

First, let's revisit Windows Activation. This was mentioned in Chapter 2, but is worth revisiting here. Most organizations tend to settle on one strategy for all clients to make life simple, instead of mixing approaches. Choose either KMS, MAK, or Active Directory activation. Try not to mix and match too much. Typically, for an AD-based network, and assuming client support, at least Windows 8.1 is required; you would use this today. Previously, many networks managed their own activation by using a KMS server. Not having a KMS server available during a deployment, or having it in a remote office, can be troublesome. It's better to leverage the nearest domain controller, which in effect all become KMS servers, eliminating a single point of failure on the network.

Be aware that activation is not just a one-time deal. For example, using KMS with remote workers can be a problem. You may have deployed new images on laptops in the corporate network, activated them, and then shipped them out to remote workers. After 180 days, activation will occur again, but what if the PC is always remote? This is something you must factor in, and a simple VPN connection may suffice, or else look at a mix of activation methods, perhaps using MAK keys for the remote PCs if connectivity to the workplace is an issue.

■ **Tip**   Get to know `slmgr.vbs`. This tool is used with volume activation and has numerous useful switches that are helpful for diagnosing activation states and issues. If you run `slmgr.vbs /dlv`, for instance, it will display the licensing state, activation count, and more, as shown in Figure 4-16. For more options, type `slmgr.vbs /?` at a command prompt. Look into `/ato` and `/rearm` especially.

Windows Script Host

Software licensing service version: 10.0.10586.0

Name: Windows(R), Enterprise edition
Description: Windows(R) Operating System, VOLUME_KMSCLIENT channel
Activation ID: 73111121-5638-40f6-bc11-f1d7b0d64300
Application ID: 55c92734-d682-4d71-983e-d6ec3f16059f
Extended PID: 03612-03290-000-000003-03-2057-10586.0000-1182016
Product Key Channel: Volume:GVLK
Installation ID:
379904383889925996144173830284794329629076232575257215361245520
Partial Product Key: 2YT43
License Status: Notification
Notification Reason: 0xC004F056.
Remaining Windows rearm count: 1001
Remaining SKU rearm count: 1001
Trusted time: 25/07/2016 06:22:05
Configured Activation Type: All
Please use slmgr.vbs /ato to activate and update KMS client information in order
to update values.

Figure 4-16. *Activation reporting with Slmgr.vbs /dlv*

Drivers

Device drivers are needed for three different phases during a deployment. Those are WinPE, setup itself, and post-installation of the operating system. Keep these as simple as possible! Do you really need that fancy driver package from the manufacturer if a standard built-in Windows driver will suffice? Do you need a video driver added in the first two phases when we are working with simple interfaces? No. Keep the specialized drivers down as far as possible, using built-in drivers wherever possible, and falling back to manufacturer drivers when you have to.

Drivers can always be added in the future through WDS and MDT to keep images valid for new hardware. This doesn't involve deploying the images, adding them, running Sysprep, and then reimaging the computer. You can add drivers offline to your images in both tools. The same can be said of updates too.

Sysprep

When running Sysprep, ensure you are using the correct version for the operating system in question; for example, the copy of Sysprep that ships with Windows 8.1 cannot be used on a Windows 10 computer and vice-versa. Sysprep generally works flawlessly, but does have logs for its actions in the different passes that it uses. You'll find these in the following areas:

- Generalize: `%Windir%|System32\Sysprep\Panther`

- Specialize: `%Windir%\Panther\`

- Unattended Windows Setup actions: `%Windir\Panther\Unattendgc`

In terms of running Sysprep, try to keep the environment as clean as possible and minimize tampering from end-user accounts. One reason for this relates to some of the built-in Store apps, such as Mail and News. If these have been removed or updated by users, Sysprep will fail, as it is expecting these to be present because they are in-box apps that come shipped with Windows 8.1 or Windows 10. This can be a show-stopping fail for Sysprep. A best practice is to always use a local administrator account to build and test the reference computer. Keep down activations as well, as mentioned earlier in this chapter.

WDS

One area of WDS to look into is prestaging clients, which will help with minimizing which clients WDS has to listen for. This involves associating a computer's MAC address, GUID, or DUID with a computer account in Active Directory. Once entered, you can specify a default WDS server and default image to the computer. This can help automate the deployment of images to known clients, and also helps prevent unknown clients from using WDS in the first place, as now the PXE response setting of the server can be changed to only respond to known computers. You can also ensure that the client resides in the correct Organization Unit in AD so that it receives the correct group policies from day one. This also means that you can use Group Policy as a way to deploy software into your image at first boot/first logon, instead of cramming it into your image.

The Iceberg of MDT

Working with MDT can be a little like seeing an iceberg. When creating task sequences, there's a heap of settings below the waterline that you may never see unless you go looking for them. Always look at the settings after running the wizard. There are so many options in there (too many to call out here) that would potentially go unnoticed if you only created a task sequence in the wizard and walked away. That would be a real shame, as there really is so much below the surface.

This also extends to the `bootstrap` and `customsettings` ini files. If you plan to use MDT half seriously, you should spend time reading up on them and experimenting with their settings to really derive the most benefit from MDT. Also, in the same vein, you may want to look at spending time learning the passes of Windows Setup and how you can automate setup.

Testing, Testing, Testing

Lots of iterative testing is required, not always because it didn't work the first time, but rather to ensure that you iron out all the wrinkles in a deployment. For example, your deployment may successfully install an operating system to a computer. Perhaps a part of it didn't work, yet it was not enough of a show-stopping event for MDT to fail the whole task. You'll certainly want to use virtual machines for testing, given their ease of reversal capability.

Dream Chasing

When building images, it is tempting to make the most perfect image possible, with the most applicable updates known to the world today. Be careful, as you can end up spending lots of time chasing the dream and never wind up deploying anything, as by the time you've parcelled everything you wanted, then put it through testing, another update comes out and you must start over again! It's OK for your image to not be 100 percent perfect. So what if a handful of updates have to be installed post-install? Is that so bad? There has to be a trade-off with perfection and what you can afford to live with in your deployment.

Summary

You've learned through the course of this chapter what lite touch means and how moving from high-touch deployment to lite touch involves many more tools and technologies. It also means more automation, and that does mean time savings. Invest the time now into learning those tools to save time later. You'll be glad you did, as it means you can reuse that knowledge over and over and apply it to other operating systems you deploy in the future.

We've covered what is involved in creating a reference computer and turning it into an image, using Sysprep along the way to generalize the machine settings. Imaging the computer using DISM on a single computer is fine, but moving that up to an Enterprise scale involves drafting in other tools, such as Windows SIM, to create answer files that automate Windows Setup and OOBE in preparation for end-user use.

Windows Deployment Services has been explained to give you the option of storing and accessing images from a network server. Taking advantage of PXE boot, modern computers can access a WDS server whenever a new image needs to be installed on a computer, or if the computer runs into problems and it would be quicker to reimage the computer back to a stable state than to spend time fixing it.

Finally, we've looked around MDT and how it can really help automate not only the stages of Windows Setup, but beyond that to add drivers, applications, and other packages to your images for more complete deployments to the desktop.

Despite this chapter focussing on lite-touch deployments, and most people using that approach to configure clean installs of operating system images, don't forget that Microsoft prefers that users upgrading to Windows 10 perform in-place upgrades, and tools like Windows SIM and MDT are geared for those scenarios as well.

In the next chapter, we will be looking at taking this a step further and building toward zero-touch deployments.

CHAPTER 5

Automating Windows Deployment with Zero Touch

In this chapter, we will be exploring how System Center Configuration Manager (SCCM) can be used to take automation of deployments to the highest possible level–that of zero touch. Simply put, this means that we can deploy an operating system and all of its applications by centrally controlling the process, without requiring any input from the end user or a technician (which would have been the case with lite touch).

Throughout this chapter, we will be building on the technologies and tools explained in Chapter 4, so everything you now know about lite touch will be put to good use here.

Note   There are several versions of System Center Configuration Manager in general use today. This includes the 2007 R3 version and the 2012 R2 version. For the purposes of this chapter, we will focus on the current one at the time of going to press, which is 2012. Most of what is covered in this chapter equally applies to all versions, but some screenshots and features and supported operating systems are different between the versions; for example, Windows 10 deployments are only supported on the 2012 version. For simplicity, we will describe the versions generically as just SCCM from now on.

Zero-touch deployments are often also known as zero-touch installations, or ZTI, just like lite touch is often known as LTI. Although the term differs, we are talking about the same thing, and the one constant is using a management tool like SCCM. Other management tools on the market offer similar features, but this chapter only shows how to achieve zero touch by using SCCM.

Overview of System Center Configuration Manager

What is System Center Configuration Manager (SCCM)?

© Chris Rhodes and Andrew Bettany 2016

C. Rhodes and A. Bettany, *Windows Installation and Update Troubleshooting*,

DOI 10.1007/978-1-4842-1827-3_5

SCCM is one of the component technologies in the Microsoft System Center suite. This includes:

- System Center Configuration Manager
- System Center Virtual Machine Manager
- System Center Operations Manager
- System Center Service Manager
- System Center Orchestrator
- System Center Data Protection Manager
- System Center App Controller
- System Center Endpoint Protection

These components can be used on their own independently or, in many cases, can be linked together and linked to other software, such as Windows ADK. SCCM itself is designed to aid the IT administrator in several ways. These include asset intelligence through client reporting of hardware and software, application and operating system delivery, and patch management.

░ **Note**   The Windows ADK is required to be installed as a prerequisite before SCCM can be installed as it requires many of the component parts, such as WinPE, USMT, and other tools that are required for operating system deployment.

The way it works is by having a central database managed by one or more servers that have clients reporting in using an installed agent. The agent needs to be installed on computers in order for them to be known to SCCM, and therefore to be able to be targeted by the administrator when an application, operating system, or setting needs to be deployed. This is undertaken silently in regards to the end user of the computer, and the agent takes care of when and how to perform the configuration change. When the changes are applied, centralized reporting at the server side can be used to view the success or failure of that change for that one computer, or across the whole environment.

A typical SCCM deployment contains several components that work together. In larger environments, these roles are found on dedicated servers, while in smaller networks some roles are found together on the same server.

Depending on the size of the network, the location of offices, clients, and other factors will determine the structure of your SCCM deployment. It's beyond the scope of this chapter to elaborate on the design of an SCCM hierarchy, but it will at least contain the following items.

Sites

- A primary site – the minimum requirement. A primary site can exist on its own or have other primary sites in the hierarchy alongside it, and can also have child secondary sites.

- Secondary sites (optional) – secondary sites relieve the burden of the client load and traffic from the primary site and allow for localization of services; for example, to account for slow WAN links. Secondary sites always include a management point and distribution point. Database replication occurs within the primary site.

Site System Servers

All servers running SCCM are regarded as site system servers and can have any of the following main roles installed (although there are more roles available):

- Site Server – first server in the site that contains the core services

- Database Server – runs SQL Server to act as the database store for SCCM data

- Management Point – main reporting point for clients when they check on their hardware and software status. Location for distribution of policies to clients.

- Distribution Point – server that maintains the applications, packages, boot files, and operating system files that will be deployed to clients

- Software Update Point – interfaces with WSUS for synchronizing software updates into SCCM, and ultimately updates to clients

---

▒ **Note**   A primary site always includes at least the site server, management point, distribution point, and site database site system roles. Other roles are optional, and not all are shown here.

Figure 5-1 shows a typical deployment scenario for a small-to-medium-sized company deployment of SCCM, utilizing a single server with all the mandatory site server roles installed.

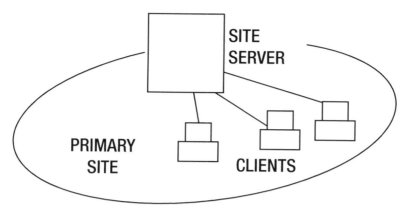

Figure 5-1. *A typical SCCM deployment*

Clients

SCCM clients are computers that have the SCCM agent installed on them. At this time, the supported list of operating systems runs from Windows XP to Windows 10, and also Windows Server 2003 and above. Interestingly, non-Microsoft operating systems such as Ubuntu and MAC OS X are also supported.

The client installs an agent that reports back inventory knowledge to the management point, and the client also receives instructions on installations and other tasks it needs to perform. Think of it like an obedient servant, always carrying out its master's instructions. The agent can perform various tasks, including applying software metering rules, asset inventory, software updates, and more.

Table 5-1 shows the different methods for installing the client agent software onto Windows computers (processes differ for Linux and Mac), including a push install method, deploying as part of an image, or by using Group Policy software installation. To some extent it doesn't matter how it gets there, as long as it does. And when it does, it will ensure the client agent starts to report in to the management point it has been told to use.

Table 5-1. *SCCM Client Installation Options*

Installation Method	Description
Manual installation	From installation media by an administrator
Client push	Uses native push method in SCCM to remotely install the agent to discovered computers
GPO	Distributes using Group Policy software installation
Software update point	Uses WSUS for installation
Logon script	Integrates install into a logon script
Upgrade	Uses SCCM software deployment to upgrade an earlier version client
Task sequence	Deploys as part of a lite- or zero-touch installation
Image deployment	Incorporates into a WIM-based deployment

Configuring OSD in System Center

You learned in Chapter 4 how MDT and Windows SIM help us to produce a healthy level of automation through task sequences and answer files, respectively. Here, we will focus on how SCCM can bring more to the table and advance that technology even further. In the language of SCCM, the process of deploying operating systems is commonly referred to as Operating System Deployment (OSD).

What Is OSD?

SCCM can be used to perform deployments from the following four scenarios:

- Image capture of a reference computer
- User state capture and restore using the User State Migration Tool (USMT)
- Operating system image deployment to a collection of computers
- Creation of task sequences (which can contain a variety of tasks)

In Figure 5-2, you can see the operating systems node in the Software Library concerning OSD. This area in the management console holds some containers that should look familiar by now, as they have overlapping features with MDT and WDS. These include:

- Drivers – downloaded device drivers imported into SCCM

- Driver packages – same as in MDT

- Operating system images – WIM files

- Operating system installers – OS ISOs for deployment

- Boot images – capture and discover WIMs added here

- Task sequences – similar to MDT task sequences

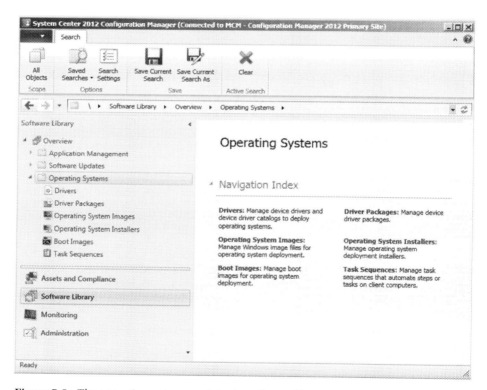

Figure 5-2. *The operating systems node in the software library*

You should by now be picking up on the fact that your knowledge of MDT and WDS is carried over here (albeit in a slightly different interface, and with further options yet to be explored at this point).

Configuring SCCM for OSD

Although support for much of the feature set required for OSD is ready to go, there is one area in particular that requires additional configuration. If you intend to use PXE boot clients to boot to SCCM, then you must install WDS on site systems that have the Distribution Point (DP) role installed, and then configure it to listen for clients (as if building a regular WDS server). This allows Configuration Manager to use the PXE listener components that are found natively in WDS.

Once WDS is installed on the DPs, support must then be enabled by clicking on the properties of the DP object, then on the PXE tab. You then configure "Enable PXE support for clients" and at least the "Allow this distribution point to respond to incoming PXE requests" option, and maybe also to respond to unknown clients, as shown in Figure 5-3. I'll note here also that adding a password can be useful to help prevent users from accidentally reimaging their PC, if the boot order becomes changed.

░ **Tip**   When making changes to a DP, such as adding an image, you are required to update the distribution point. This is necessary to ensure that the files can be found on the DP, ready for clients to use. This is achieved by choosing the option to distribute content. You then choose which DPs (or DP groups) will receive the files. This must be done in advance of deploying this to clients, and it can take time to distribute multi-gigabyte files.

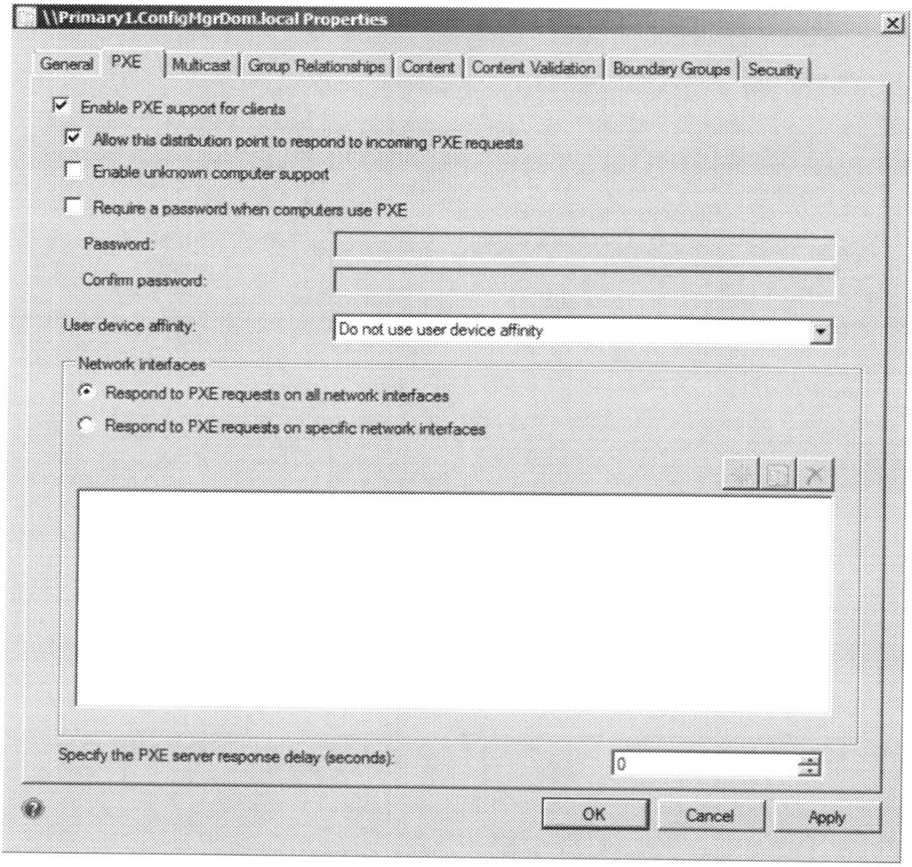

Figure 5-3. *Configuring PXE support on a Distribution Point site server*

The next steps to configuring OSD support are similar to how WDS is configured–images are required. Images are, of course, boot images and installation images. Just like with WDS, you could add some default images from installation media like Windows ISOs, or you could custom create your own with the ADK tools. When it comes to installation images, you could actually use SCCM to create a deployment task sequence that captures an existing computer, including the Sysprep stage and capture process. Alternatively, if you manually created an image using DISM, you could also add this here too.

Images are required for the next steps in the process, which is to distribute images to client computers using either lite- or zero-touch methods. This will be explained in the next section.

Integrating MDT with System Center

Although task sequences appear in the software library, as you saw in Figure 5-2, full MDT functionality is not present by default. You can work with the task sequences node in the library and create task sequences that deploy an operating system image, or that deploy and capture a reference machine, for instance, but it's not the same as actually using MDT, although there are many crossovers.

To get the most out of task sequences and deployment in general in SCCM, you should install the latest copy of MDT into your environment. This brings around 280 enhancements to the standard feature set. You integrate MDT and SCCM by installing MDT on a computer that has the SCCM management tools installed (typically your admin workstation where you will be creating task sequences). Once this has completed, from the Start Menu on that computer, load the `Configure ConfigMgr Integration` application that got installed with MDT. This tool integrates the two technologies. You need to identify the site server name and site code, as shown in Figure 5-4, to get it configured.

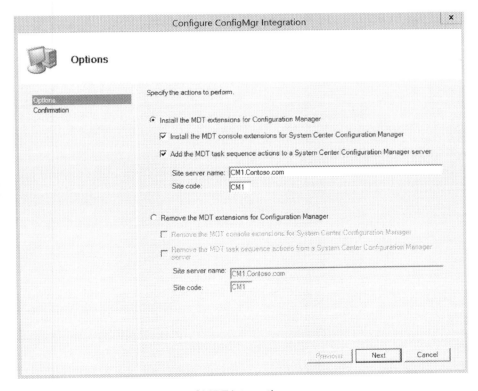

Figure 5-4. Configuring SCCM and MDT integration

Now that this is installed, reopen the SCCM management console, where new options will be available, such as Create MDT Task Sequence, as shown in Figure 5-5.

Figure 5-5. *MDT Task Sequences in SCCM*

MDT task sequences parallel the functionality you would expect to see in the MDT Deployment Workbench, but the benefit here is the ability to leverage the extra capabilities of SCCM for deployment. You may recall from Chapter 4 that MDT has various task sequences and that SCCM natively does as well. Table 5-2 summarizes the choices available.

Table 5-2. *Microsoft Deployment Toolkit Task Sequences*

MDT Task Sequence Name	SCCM Task Sequence Name	MDT & SCCM Integrated Task Sequence Name
Sysprep and capture	Install an existing image package	Client task sequence
Standard client task sequence	Build and capture a reference o/s image	Client replace task sequence
Standard client replace task sequence	Install an existing image package to a virtual hard drive	Microsoft deployment custom task sequence
Standard client upgrade task sequence	Custom task sequence	Server task sequence
Custom task sequence		User-driven installation replace task sequence
Lite-touch OEM task sequence		
Standard server task sequence		
Standard server upgrade task sequence		
Post OS installation task sequence		
Deploy to VHD client task sequence		
Deploy to VHD server task sequence		

So, on the face of it, MDT has the widest range of choices for task sequences. One thing to note, however, is that the integrated task sequences in SCCM all take shape based on the same set of choices, and although they appear differently, they still have options that parallel MDT task sequences. An example of this can be seen in Figure 5-6, where there is the option to capture an image as part of the sequence or to skip the capture and deploy only.

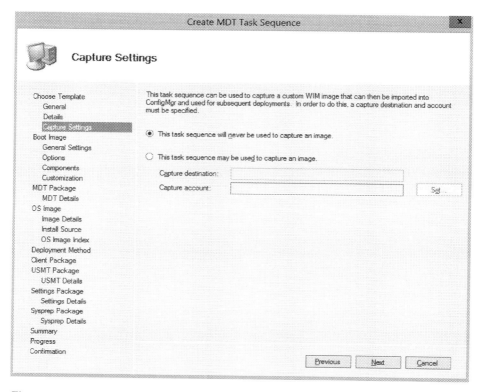

Figure 5-6. Integrated SCCM/MDT task sequences

Of course, the whole point of SCCM deployments is to take advantage of zero-touch installations. This is where the task sequences in SCCM really come into their own. To make a task sequence zero touch, there are two main areas to configure. You can see in Figure 5-6 the step named Deployment Method, which is where you are prompted if you would like the task sequence to be zero touch or user driven (a.k.a., lite touch). If you choose zero touch, the task sequence prompts for input for the settings package, as shown in Figure 5-7.

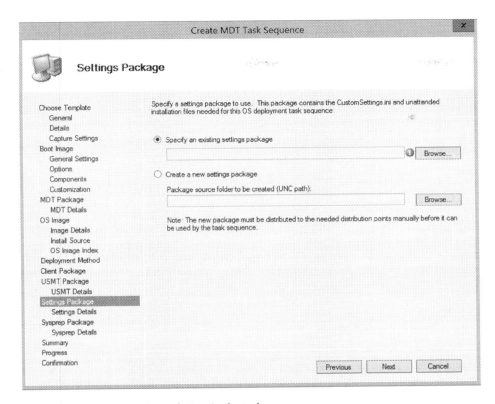

Figure 5-7. Settings package choices in the task sequence

At this stage you can point to a settings package you have already created or you can have it generate one for you. This creates an answer file for setup and a customsettings.ini file. Each has default choices (mostly in the answer file) that remove the need for any user input at all when the task sequence is being deployed to clients, when running Windows setup on the target computers.

This is another example of where the ADK tools are being used under the hood for you, and a level of abstraction from those is being achieved in SCCM. Another area where MDT integration brings more to the table in SCCM is when you edit the task sequence after creation. This gives a very wide range of options for extra customization, including a specific menu of options from MDT, as shown in Figure 5-8.

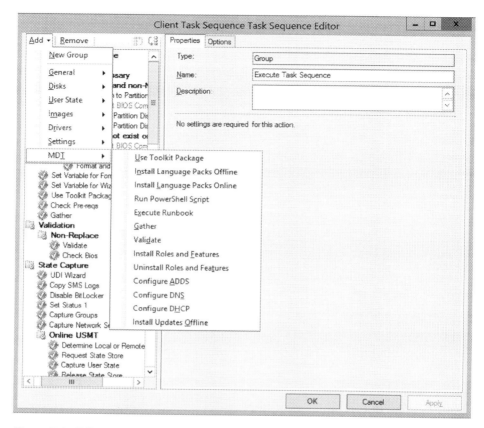

Figure 5-8. *Editing a task sequence and adding MDT steps*

Some great examples of this are adding PowerShell scripts (which could basically be doing almost anything, so it extends the scope of the task sequence almost infinitely) and some useful components like adding language packs, which is useful when you have multi-language deployments of an image.

Once you have created a task sequence, you can deploy this to a collection. Collections are groups of computers that you create in SCCM. These can have a direct membership (like a static membership) or be based on a dynamic membership; for instance, the "All Windows 7 computers" option has a rule that checks the operating system version. There are some default collections in SCCM, but usually administrators will want to create several of their own.

To deploy the task sequence, you will use the "Deploy Software Wizard" option by selecting the object and selecting the "Deploy" option for it. This then asks you which collections you would like to distribute it to and whether this is a required or optional deployment. You can see some of these settings in Figure 5-9. Required deployments are useful when you want to ensure that all computers in a group or department are deployed at the same time, such as overnight. You also have the option of scheduling the deployment, and even using "wake-on" LAN functionality to wake systems up at night and install the package before shutting the system down again.

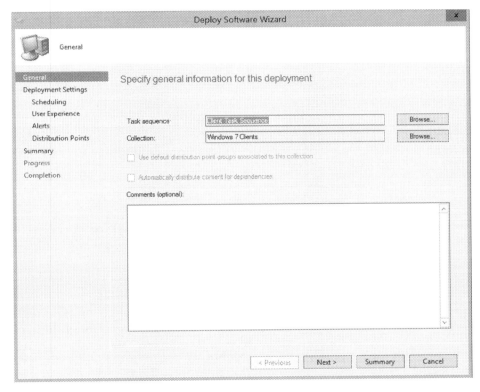

Figure 5-9. Deploying a task sequence to a collection

To summarize the process end to end of creating a zero-touch installation, a high-level overview version of the steps is presented here:

1. After installing SCCM, install WDS and configure PXE boot if required.

2. Install MDT and integrate MDT with SCCM.

3. Create new task sequence(s).

4. Choose to install an image with the option of capturing the source computer first, and also backing up and restoring user state with USMT.

5. Ensure that zero touch is selected and a settings package removes user input.

6. Edit the task sequence for further customization.

7. Include updates, applications, and the SCCM client installation package.

8. Distribute content to distribution point(s).

9. Deploy to collection(s).

10. Verify success using the reporting functions of SCCM.

Monitoring and Troubleshooting Zero Touch

So, with all this enterprise software in SCCM, layered upon the Windows ADK, resting on a SQL Server database, and augmented with WDS and MDT, what can possibly go wrong?!

Clearly there are many moving parts to this machine. No longer do we have an application like Windows SIM creating answer files that are used in a lite-touch installation of Windows. SCCM brings a world of asset intelligence, reporting, and new methods of installing operating system images. A working knowledge of how System Center Configuration Manager works is really needed in order to troubleshoot it effectively. While that may be beyond the scope of this chapter, this section will give you some pointers and tips to help you troubleshoot your zero-touch installations.

Distribution Points

There are several reasons why a deployment may fail because of distribution points. Some are more straightforward than others. The main tip is to ensure that the distribution point(s) have been updated. You can choose which DPs get copies of the files that make up your task sequence, which includes the installation and boot images. It's not necessarily the case that all DPs have the ability to serve clients with your images, as you may not have included them all when distributing the content. You should check which DP(s) are configured to receive your task sequence and change it as needed to include other DPs that serve affected clients.

> ▓ **Tip** Consider using fallback DPs as well to avoid clients' not installing due to their preferred DPs not being available or not storing the content in the first place.

You can also run into issues where remote clients do not install the task sequence. This is actually a setting on the task sequence that can be enabled or disabled for remote clients. The default is that they would not install it.

Don't forget also that shifting multiple GB images does take time, and you need to be patient to let that happen before deploying the OSD task to clients. You can use the console to check on the status of this before starting a deployment. If a DP is being updated when you begin a deployment, that deployment will fail with an error.

> ▓ **Tip** SCCM 2012 R2 now has the ability to deploy cloud-based distribution points that are intended to serve remote workers by using Microsoft Azure–based DPs. This can help solve issues related to not finding the closest site correctly or a lack of bandwidth, especially with OSD deployments.

Logs

During a task sequence, the client writes to a log file named SMSTS.log. Depending on where in the sequence it is, the file may be in one of several different places on the machine. For instance, it resides in x:\windows\temp\smstslog\smsts.log during the PXE stage. At the end of the process, it can be found in C:\windows\system32\ccm\logs. This is the main log and is the most important one to start with for troubleshooting task sequences specifically, but it's worth noting that there are literally dozens of log files in SCCM that can help to diagnose faults across all aspects of the product.

Monitoring

With zero touch, the whole point is that no one needs to be there to babysit the installation process. This begs the question: how can you tell it worked? SCCM has a rich reporting feature set for you to see what is going on at any point. Here's a few areas to look at to help assist you in understanding which clients have/have not received an operating system:

- With MDT integration, real-time monitoring data can be viewed from within the MDT Deployment Workbench. In the Deployment Workbench, expand MDT Production and look at the Monitoring node. This will show the progress of the deployment process.

- You can also check the Deployments node in the Monitoring area of the SCCM Management Console to check on the overall status (compliance) of computers that should have processed the installation.

- Reports in the Monitoring area in the console can be used in conjunction with SQL Server Reporting Services to create and run reports on all kinds of aspects of SCCM, including OSD.

Task Sequences

A few simple things to check in task sequences often show you missed options. Check the following:

- Does the task sequence list the package as *required* or *available*? If *required*, then clients should process it if it applies to their collection. If it's *available*, then the default is not to install it, but rather to offer it optionally.

- Did you use a settings package, and does it contain all the customization necessary to fully complete an installation without user input? There are so many settings that can be configured in customsettings.ini, and you will need to validate that the data is good, no typos of course, and that it adheres to the format that it is expecting.

- If you are not sure where a task sequence is failing, configure the task sequence so that it is visible to the end user so you can interactively view which step is failing. This is really useful during testing when bottoming-out issues.

Clients

There are all sorts of reasons why a client doesn't successfully get installed. One quick check is to see which collection(s) the client belongs to. Don't forget–some collections may be using a dynamic membership that uses a query to determine membership, so just because PC1 was a member of Collection1 yesterday doesn't mean it is today. You can add and remove PCs from collections as needed.

Generally speaking, the SCCM agent on a client is fairly bulletproof, and you should resist uninstalling it and reinstalling it in an attempt to solve problems. This doesn't usually solve them anyway, as typically problems are not on the client itself.

▓ **Tip** On boot images, enable support for the Windows command prompt by configuring the Customization tab on the boot images. This will allow a technician to press F8 during OSD deployment on a client for troubleshooting anything locally outside of the OSD processes, such as running Diskpart, IPConfig, or other command-line tools.

Clients can fail to connect to the PXE server during boot. Check the obvious things, like whether the DHCP server has enough spare addresses. But also look into whether you have a network admin account created for the PXE clients so as to be able to connect to SCCM from bare-metal installs. By default, this will need to be created from scratch, so PXE boots don't work out of the box.

Check to see if the necessary drivers are present in your images. You will need, as a minimum, network card drivers for WinPE and the installation phases. This may involve adding the same drivers twice over.

Summary

In this chapter, you have learned how to create zero-touch deployments (often known as ZTI). Layering System Center Configuration Manager onto the Windows ADK can help you create task sequences more easily and with a greater depth of settings for either lite-touch or zero-touch installations. SCCM also goes beyond deploying the operating system and applications though, as it is an enterprise-class product that can be used to collect hardware and software inventory information, deploy configuration settings and applications, and also meter their use. We've really only skimmed the surface of SCCM's capabilities in this chapter, and perhaps this may inspire you to find out more.

More important, though, this chapter has sought to educate you in how to create zero-touch deployments so you are able to move task sequences you learned about in Chapter 4 using MDT on its own up to the next level and be able to instruct entire collections of computers that they need to install your task sequence at a time of your choosing. You will need to experiment with the capabilities you have learned here and create a test lab where you can build and trash, many times over, the environment in order to be fully confident that your task sequence can be deployed to 10,000 computers hands-free!

CHAPTER 6

▓ ▓ ▓

Updating and Maintaining Windows

Why bother? It worked when it left the factory, didn't it?

Operating systems today are more complex than ever before. The sheer amount of lines of code that goes into making an operating system (OS) runs into the millions. There is going to be the occasional bug that needs fixing, but updates are more than just bug fixes. Modern operating systems receive updates that cover a range of different areas, which will be explored in this chapter.

One thing that needs to be understood early on is that applying updates is very much a facet of supporting modern operating systems (and not just Windows). Understanding how and why updates are applied and the infrastructure that supports this is vital to ensuring that computers are up to date and continue to function correctly.

This is, in fact, no different than other technologies we consume in our everyday lives. Car engine management systems, smart TVs, set-top boxes, and more all use this same principle, and if you think about it, it makes sense. Updating your TV or set-top box allows you to discover new channels or content not previously available to you. Updating your car allows for better engine and fuel performance based on field data collected from hundreds of cars driving millions of miles.

Failure to update computers is not really an option in today's world. If a vulnerability exists, has been identified, and has had a fix put out, then there is a duty of care by the IT professional to ensure that the computers that they look after get that update installed as quickly as possible. That said, there is a trade-off between getting a machine up to date as promptly as possible and the need to pause and reflect on the potential negative impact that could occur if the update fails and puts the machine into a non-working state.

In this chapter, we will explore these issues and learn how Windows can be configured appropriately and how Windows Server Update Services (WSUS) can be employed to control how and when updates are deployed in an organization.

Updates vs. Upgrades

Before you learn more about how to configure updates, it's important to understand the difference between updates and upgrades and the different types of updates available to install.

© Chris Rhodes and Andrew Bettany 2016
C. Rhodes and A. Bettany, *Windows Installation and Update Troubleshooting*,
DOI 10.1007/978-1-4842-1827-3_6

Updates (commonly described as *patches*) fall into several different classifications. Not all of these are patches (or fixes), which it is why it's not accurate to describe them as such. Table 6-1 describes the different kinds of updates available.

Table 6-1. *Update Configuration Options*

Update Type	Explanation
Critical Update	A fix that addresses a non-security-related critical bug
Definition Update	Anti-malware or anti-virus definition update for Windows Defender
Drivers	Hardware device drivers
Feature Packs	New feature release rolled into a product
Security Updates	Fix that addresses a security-related vulnerability
Service Packs	Cumulative set of combined updates that can be installed as one to save time and provides a measured level of compliance. Often also contains new features.
Tools	Utility or set of tools
Update Rollups	Like a smaller scale service pack, contains a cumulative set of updates to install as a single entity to save time and provides a measured level of compliance
Updates	Anything else not covered by security updates, critical updates, or other category to provide a fix for a specific issue
Upgrades	New builds of Windows that bring new features and fixes

As you can see, there's a spread of different updates. Some are released almost daily, as in the case of definition updates, and some on a much slower release cycle, such as service packs or update rollups. It's worth noting that some types of updates have over time become less important. Service packs (SPs) are a prime example of this.

Going back over historical service packs, there has been a shift from fewer service packs, where customers would often hold off deploying updates individually and deploy a service pack once a year or so instead, to a release cadence where Microsoft has stopped entirely in favour of smaller incremental updates or using the update rollup approach to allow customers to milestone their release internally. As you can see from Table 6-2, that changeover is now complete.

Table 6-2. *Service Packs*

Operating System	Final Service Pack
Windows NT 4.0	6a
Windows Server 2000	4
Windows Server 2003	2
Windows XP	3
Windows Vista / Windows Server 2008	2
Windows Server 2008 R2 / Windows 7	1
Windows Server 2012 / Windows 8	None
Windows Server 2012 R2 / Windows 8.1	None
Windows 10	None

Upgrades (not to be confused with updates), describe whole new builds of Windows that are released that contain new features. So, these are not really about bug fixes, but more about delivery of new functionality to the operating system through feature enhancements of existing apps/technologies or the addition of entirely brand new features.

Configuring Windows Update

Since Windows 95, Microsoft has offered a service through which customers can receive updates to their operating systems, and more recently other apps such as Office applications. This was previously known as Windows Update, but later became known as Microsoft Update (incorporating the updates to Office and other products). Within Windows itself, there is a way to configure how Windows updates, and the feature is known as Windows Update in the Control Panel, as shown in Figure 6-1, a screenshot taken from a Windows 8.1 computer.

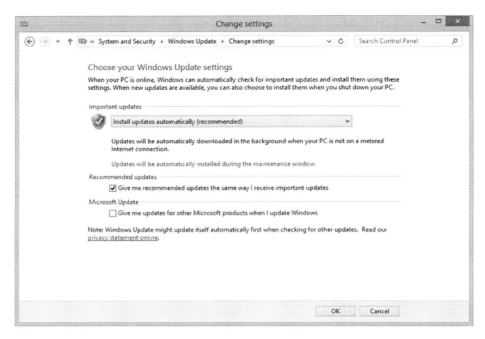

Figure 6-1. *Windows Update in the Control Panel*

Assuming for now that a computer is using the Microsoft Update location for updates, and not WSUS, there are a few options can be configured around how it works, such as how to download and install updates. These options are summarized in Table 6-3.

Table 6-3. *Update Configuration Options*

Option	Explanation
Install updates automatically (recommended)	This is really the no-brainer option, and it's also the default. This will check for updates on a cyclical basis, download them, and then install them without interaction. This is really the best option for 99 percent of computers.
Download updates but let me choose whether to install them	Not a bad option, as it checks automatically for needed updates and will download them to the local drive, ready for installation. However, it won't actually install updates until the administrator of the computer has consented to that.
Check for updates but let me choose whether to download and install them	Similar to preceding option, but the decision of whether to download is also placed in the hands of the administrator.
Never check for updates (not recommended)	This is for the minority of cases where either an alternative update strategy (e.g., manual installation approach) is employed or there is no reason to install updates, such as for a test virtual machine that does not have network access.

Clearly Microsoft has a preference for Windows machines, and the naming gives that away. But let's reflect on these options. Installing updates automatically seems to make perfect sense, as this is really a case of "let the computer get on with it." So why would you not want this? There are some situations where going "off-grid" makes sense. Some computers will never connect to the Internet, or even to any network. There are standalone computers that run factory floor–type applications that are not networked, or virtual machine–based installations of Windows that are connected to private networks or no network at all.

The other two options are halfway houses that can potentially leave computers in a less than ideal state. If the computer, for example, is configured to download updates, but to wait for an administrator to approve the installation, invariably the user will postpone the install, as they are permitted to do so, because, by definition, they are using the computer and will most likely not want to be distracted by the installation or a possible reboot following it. The option to notify for download first also compounds that issue, leading to situations where computers are not compliant for varying lengths of time–or worse, computers that do not get the necessary updates installed at all.

In other words, leaving matters in the hands of the end user may not be such a great idea, as across a network, a systems administrator will not have an easy way of knowing the overall state of computers without visiting them individually or relying on other tools, such as System Center Configuration Manager or Microsoft Intune.

The remaining options in the user interface are more straightforward. Selecting "Recommended updates" ensures that computers receive lower-tier updates that are not flagged as critical or security. The different types of updates will be explored later in this chapter.

Windows 10 computers have a different interface for configuration, but the options are broadly similar. Figure 6-2 shows the configuration options for Windows 10 using the new Settings app, rather than Control Panel, which was used in previous versions of Windows.

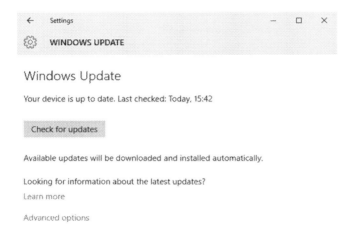

Figure 6-2. *Windows 10 update settings*

You'll notice that the main options are essentially hidden away from the main view here, and that's intentional. Microsoft has taken a much different angle on updates (and, for that matter, upgrades) in Windows 10. Most users won't go beyond this screen, where they can check for updates and see when the update check was last performed.

It's only when you dig a bit deeper that the advanced settings uncover more about how it works. You can configure Windows 10 for "Automatic (recommended)" or, as Figure 6-3 shows, "Notify to schedule restart." So, in other words, you *can't* postpone the download or the installation in the same way as before.

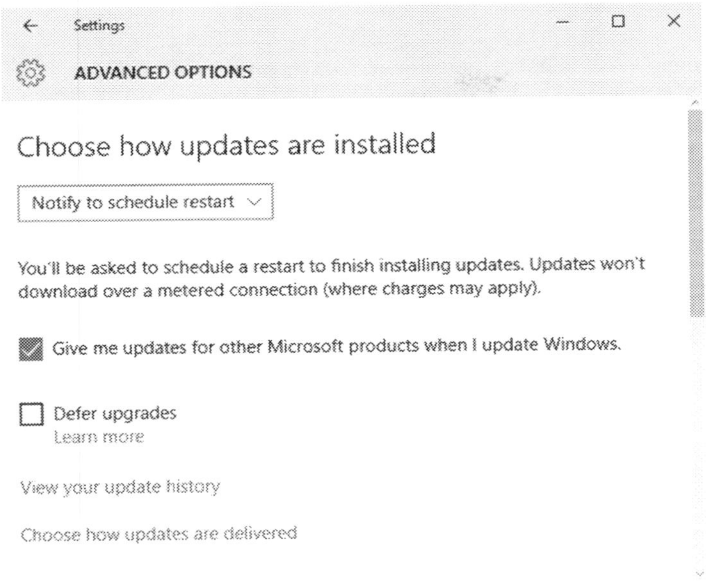

Figure 6-3. *Advanced Windows 10 settings*

This is a significant shift in direction, with the upshot being that Microsoft should be better able to ensure that computers are receiving their updates more quickly and more consistently. This is beneficial going forward, as computers across the world will be more in step with one another, and there will not be as big a lag between managed devices that are up to date and computers where it is not seen as important to be kept up to date. There are exceptions to this, such as offline computers, ATMs, and other line-of-business computers that cannot be connected to the Internet.

Also within the advanced options are options to defer upgrades (note the word *upgrades*, not updates) and the ability to store updates on your computer for others to use, and likewise to be able to obtain updates from other computers on your network. For home networks or workgroups without WSUS servers, it is a great idea to be able to cache bits to reduce the bandwidth used for common updates that would otherwise have to be downloaded multiple times on the same network. You can even configure Windows to solely obtain updates from local network computers. So, for example, in a small network one computer can be designated to download the updates from Microsoft Update online, and the rest can stream from this computer.

The ability to receive updates for other products that are curated by Microsoft Update is also a benefit, especially when using products such as Microsoft Office. Originally, Office updates were provided separately, but it makes sense to create a more seamless experience for the end user where all major software, not just the operating system, is covered by the same update process. This can also include software that accompanies devices, such as mouse driver applications and other driver packages.

Services

It's important at this point to explain that there are a couple of services in Windows that control how Windows Update works. First, there is the Windows Update service, which does the heavy lifting of checking which updates are installed locally, checking against the database of what is available, downloading, installing, and reporting on the state of updates. This is clearly the main component for operations. It is supplemented by the Background Intelligent Transfer Service (or BITS). This is a dependency service for Windows Update, so both need to be running for updates to work. We'll cover more on this in the troubleshooting section later.

Windows 10

With Windows 10, Microsoft has taken a very different view of updates and upgrades, as alluded to previously. This has a *big* impact on how you choose to update PCs going forward, so it's worth spending some time examining what the options are. Let's start by looking at the way versioning works.

We've already seen how the concept of service packs has vanished. In the past, service packs gave many organizations an excuse for delaying their deployments of Windows until a perceived stable level was reached. Taking this to the extreme, Microsoft has announced that Windows 10 will be the last version of Windows that they produce, and they will instead move to an update cadence of a continuously updating model, so versioning becomes less relevant. This brings Windows in line with other software, such as smartphone apps, where consumers do not expect a one-off development of code, but rather a constant tweaking and improvement.

So, how does that work?

As you saw in Chapter 3, Windows 10 devices will fall into one of four main categories, which Microsoft calls servicing models. These servicing models distribute new operating system *upgrades*. These are summarized in Table 6-4.

Table 6-4. *Windows 10 Servicing Models*

Servicing Model	Explanation
Windows Insider Preview Program	Designed for early adopters, software developers, and enthusiasts who want cutting-edge builds delivered as soon as possible in order to test and evaluate new features. Carries more risk than other models, but ensures the most up to date state of features.
Current Branch (CB)	The bulk of computers worldwide fit into this category. Consumer PCs and devices will use this as their default, and it cannot be disabled on Home edition. The mainstream option.
Current Branch for Business (CBB)	Includes Pro, Enterprise, and Education editions. Allows organizations the ability to defer upgrades up to four months.
Long-Term Servicing Branch (LTSB)	For computers that run mission-critical applications where up-to-dateness is not required for greater long-term predictability of build state. Lacks Edge browser, Windows Store, Cortana, and other preinstalled universal apps. Uses a specific SKU variant of Enterprise edition named Enterprise LTSB.

Drilling into these a little further is necessary, as they are less widely understood because Windows 10 is relatively new, despite the growing installed base. Microsoft introduced the Windows Insider program while Windows 10 was in development to allow users to sample a development version of the product (what would in the past have been called a beta). Millions of people took Microsoft up on this. There are always going to be people who want the latest and greatest, either to be ahead of the curve with new technology from an enthusiast perspective or because they will be supporting Windows or applications that use Windows with this in the future.

The *Insider* program allowed Microsoft to receive a massive amount of telemetry data back on how users were using Windows, and also on what worked or what didn't work, in order to help fine tune Windows 10 for its eventual release. This worked out so successfully, that Microsoft decided to continue the program even after Windows 10 was released to the public at large. Users can opt-in their PC to being part of the Insider Program using the Settings app in Windows 10, as shown in Figure 6-4. It is not a permanent change, as it is reversible, but users in the Insider Program must be aware that this carries some risk, as they are using builds that have not had much real-world "air time" outside of being developed and deployed at Microsoft. This is really Microsoft allowing early adopters to test the waters and be a first wave of public testers. *Only enable this feature on a test computer or if you are happy to bear the risk and take regular backups of data.*

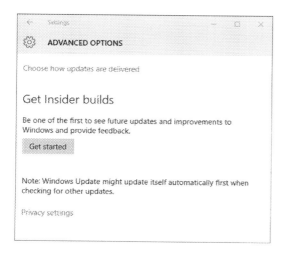

Figure 6-4. *Enabling Insider builds*

Within the Insider program there are two "rings": fast and slow. These rings dictate how frequently your computer receives new builds that are published to the Internet for computers that have opted in. You can almost think of it as cutting edge and not-quite-so cutting edge, but still ahead of the curve. You can switch between these at any time in the Settings app after configuring it for first use.

■ **Note**   Insider builds are sourced from Windows Update on the Internet, so are not applicable for distribution from a WSUS server. Signing up for Insider builds requires signing in with a Microsoft account.

Current Branch (CB) is expected to be adopted by most small- to medium-sized organizations and consumer devices. This will result in hundreds of millions of devices at pretty much the same build level as one another at any given point in time. This distribution of builds ensures that the widest and most diverse set of computer hardware and industries is running these builds. If anything goes awry, it will be quickly spotted by the telemetry data (although in theory this should not occur due to tens of millions of Insider computers having run these first).

Computers using Current Branch cannot decide when they will receive builds if they are obtaining updates from Windows Update. This means that the main installed base of Windows 10 computers (especially in the consumer space) will be aligned with one another. Administrators who manage computers using WSUS have more control over their distribution, which will be explained shortly.

Current Branch for Business (CBB)–enabled computers are essentially the same as CB computers, but with the option to defer the upgrades component. This option is only available to the following editions of Windows: Pro, Education, Enterprise, Mobile Enterprise, and IoT Core Pro.

To configure one of the eligible editions for CBB, you need to configure either the Settings app or Group Policy settings, as shown in Figure 6-5.

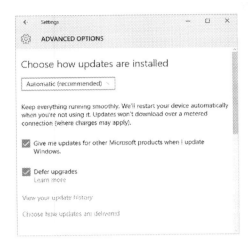

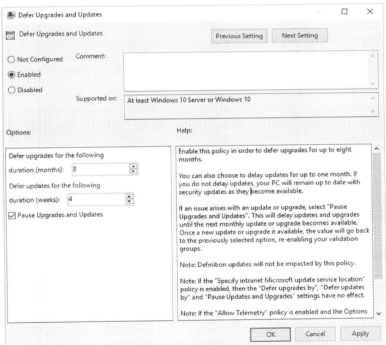

Figure 6-5. *Enabling Current Branch for Business*

You can see from Figure 6-5 that in the Settings app you can only set the option to defer upgrades (with no value for the period possible). In Group Policy, however, you can fine tune the settings and configure the value for upgrades to a maximum of eight months, and one month for updates. So, essentially, a computer can be kept reasonably up to date for security updates and other fixes, but lag by up to eight months on new builds that deliver added functionality.

▓ **Note**   When an organization configures some or all of its computer in this way, it is said to have deployed **Windows Update for Business.** In reality, all you are doing is configuring the deferral options, rather than deploying a service as the name may suggest.

The *Long-Term Servicing Branch* is the final servicing model and is aimed at a completely different use-case scenario. While it should be observed that having updated or upgraded computers overall is a good thing, and having harmony worldwide makes it easier for Microsoft and organizations to support, there are some exceptions to this. Consider a computer that resides on a factory floor and runs a production process in a plant that runs 24/7. Or a computer in a hospital that only manages a piece of medical equipment. It's likely that these computers are classed as mission critical in their own way, but equally they can be regarded as single-use devices that run a specific workload. The computers may never be connected to a network, much less the Internet, so the relevance of keeping these kinds of computers up to date becomes somewhat nonexistent–as long as Windows runs reliably, of course.

Administrators who maintain these types of computers usually want to balance a computer's pace of updates with the need to keep the computer up as long as possible in a stable state without the added complications of untested updates interfering.

Recognizing this type of scenario, Microsoft has made available a different edition of Windows 10 that uses this longer term servicing model entirely, known as Windows 10 Enterprise LTSB. This is only available to education and enterprise customers and cannot be easily switched to without (re)installing the entire operating system, so it needs to be carefully planned and used on a case by case basis in an organization.

It's possible to have computers in an organization belonging to any combination of the four servicing models. At any given point, within each model, there can be computers that are also said to belong to different "branches" of servicing depending on how the administrator has set the computer up.

Let's have a look at how that might work for a fictitious company that has 1,000 computers. Consider that, all things being equal, the company understands the importance of maintaining up-to-date computers and has a proactive policy on managing updates. Most computers would be configured to use Current Branch and, due to the size of the company, most likely would be deploying updates using WSUS. These computers would be serviced according to the way in which the administrator has deployed WSUS on the network. There could, for instance, be some computers that update more frequently than others, or some that get updated manually.

There may also be some computers that software developers use to test new applications. These applications may require access to the latest builds to ensure that the developers can check application compatibility across any new builds that their customers may be using. These computers may use Insider Program builds, but some computers may use the slow ring and some the fast ring branches. So, at any given point in time, there are some computers using the very latest build available and some that lag by a few days or weeks to allow for comprehensive testing with a semi-stable release that won't be updated too frequently.

Other computers on the network may be deemed mission critical, and the administrators may want to mitigate some risk by effectively creating groups of computers that have deferred options set (a.k.a. Current Branch for Business). Within this subset of computers using CBB, there could be some computers being serviced with updates lagging by two weeks, some by three weeks, and some by four weeks. The same could be true for upgrades (new builds) as well, so some could lag by four months or eight months.

The servicing branch is therefore dictated by the build that the computer is on and the updates configuration that services that build at a given point. So, Computer1 may be using build 1025, with no delay in receiving updates. Computer2 may be using build 1000 with no delay in receiving updates either, but those updates are relevant to build 1000, not 1025. That said, there will be some updates, like regular Windows Defender malware definitions, that would be the same on both computers.

Setting Up and Managing WSUS

In the early days of Microsoft Update, administrators lacked the tools to control the distribution of updates to computers that they managed. Much less so, administrators also did not have insight into the state of compliance of their computers in regards to their update state. The larger the size of the network, the more this problem was compounded.

Administrators turned to Microsoft and third parties to come up with a solution. Originally, Microsoft lacked the tools, and the third-party market helped develop a solution. Microsoft eventually took this on in its own right as the service that has become WSUS. It was a company called Shavlik Technologies that produced a tool called HFNetChk (short for HotFix Network Checker) in 2001 that started the ball rolling, which then led to Microsoft releasing a tool called MBSA (Microsoft Baseline Security Analyzer). The premise of both tools was a way for administrators to assess the update state of the computers that they managed on their network (rather than individually).

▓ **Note** Hot fix is the name given to a specific type of update that customers used to request outside of the normal channel of update distribution to fix specific issues in the field on Microsoft technologies like Windows Server, SQL Server, and Exchange Server. These days the term is less used as customers are more aligned to having the term *update* cover the different varieties discussed at the beginning of this chapter. Likewise, the term *patch* is usually referred to in a generic sense by administrators implying any type of update, but it remains in use as a slang term.

From these roots, SUS (Software Update Services), later WSUS (Windows Server Update Services), was born. This integrated service allows administrators to control the release of updates of all kinds to the computers on their networks, with the added intelligence of update-by-update or computer-by-computer reporting (which will be covered later). WSUS is widely used in small-, medium-, and large-sized organizations. It is often used in conjunction with System Center Configuration Manager in larger enterprise networks. It is beyond the scope of this chapter to show that integration here, but the principles of how WSUS works there is reflected in the System Center tools.

In a typical basic deployment that a small- or medium-sized organization would use, the architecture of a WSUS infrastructure would look like the one in Figure 6-6. Here, you can see that a single WSUS server deployed behind the corporate edge firewall (but not typically in a perimeter network) would be used to connect to Microsoft Update online, synchronize the content, and control the update distribution for the connected clients that are configured to use it. Note that not all computers on the network have to be configured to use WSUS just because it is there.

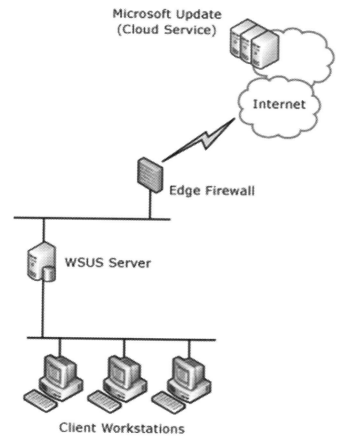

Figure 6-6. *A basic WSUS infrastructure*

Installing and Configuring WSUS

WSUS is now an integral part of the Windows Server operating system family of product, far from its origins as a downloadable add-on for Windows Server 2003. It is installed as a role in Windows Server 2012 R2, as shown in Figure 6-7. The server running WSUS requires at least 2 GB RAM over the minimum for Windows Server, plus enough disk space to store the amount of updates that the administrator chooses to cache from the Internet. A recommended starting point is 50 GB to 100 GB. The actual amount depends on the types of update classifications, products covered, and language iterations of the updates stored locally.

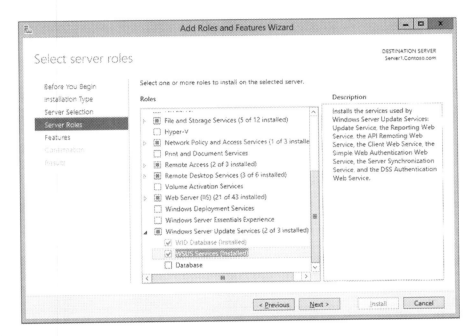

Figure 6-7. *Installing WSUS*

Regardless of the version of Windows Server that WSUS is deployed to, a common requirement is that a database must be used in support of the server. That database can be a SQL Server database on the same or a separate server, or a Windows Internal Database (WID), which can be installed as shown in the previous figure. For smaller scale networks or for testing, a WID is recommended.

There are other scenarios in which WSUS can be deployed, and the most common other way is as a hierarchy of servers. This would suit a network that consisted of a main office and multiple regional or branch offices where centralized control would achieve consistency and ease of management instead of managing a series of independent WSUS servers, for example.

The benefits of a hierarchy include minimizing the amount of times that an update needs to be downloaded from the Internet, hosting updates physically close to the clients, and synchronizing update approval states for updates across sites.

When WSUS is deployed in a hierarchy, administrators can choose to have the servers configured in either replica mode or autonomous mode, as shown in Figure 6-8.

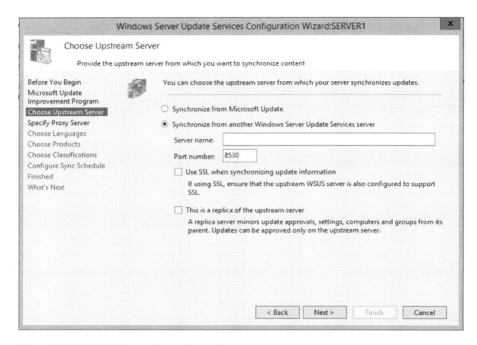

Figure 6-8. *WSUS hierarchy configuration*

In replica mode, all the update approval settings, computers, and other settings are mirrored from the upstream server. This simplifies administration in an organization that needs the consistency of a parallel configuration across sites to ensure that computers that are serviced by WSUS meet compliance settings. The other way that a hierarchy can be configured is in autonomous mode, where the upstream server is used purely as a synchronization point for the updates themselves rather than using the Internet directly. In this mode, the downstream server administrator can control how and when updates get distributed without regard to how the upstream server is configured.

It is worth noting that there other options for WSUS server configurations, such as with load-balanced clusters or by not caching the updates from the Internet but rather leaving the download of updates to the client to perform independently. This is good when the connection from the client to the WSUS server is poor compared to the client's connection to the Internet.

Other options that are defined during setup of WSUS include the schedule (a time once a day or at night is selected) for when to synchronize from Microsoft Update and the products and classifications to sync.

▦ **Tip** When WSUS syncs with Microsoft Update, it also syncs the published catalog of updates. When configuring WSUS for the first time, it's a good idea to allow WSUS to sync once with only a very small set of products and classifications selected in order for it to obtain the most up-to-date list of products and categories from the catalog, from which you can choose later. For example, with the version of WSUS included with Windows Server 2012 R2, there is no in-box knowledge of Windows 10 operating systems until the first sync.

It's also very important to note that WSUS needs to update itself to provide support for Windows 10 feature upgrades, an update that is installed as described here: https://support.microsoft.com/en-us/kb/3095113.

Approving Updates

A key area in WSUS configuration is setting how and when to approve updates for installation on connected clients. Just because a client is configured to point to the WSUS server and the server has recently synced new content, it does not mean that the client will receive many updates. An administrator must decide how this should occur.

This decision can be different for different sets of computers, known as *computer groups* in WSUS. For example, for Windows client operating systems it may be a good idea to automatically download and install updates without prior testing in an environment if testing is not possible due to resource constraints or attitude to risk. For server operating systems, it may be decided to not automatically install updates at all, and instead have them installed manually during a maintenance window to prevent unscheduled downtime. Alternatively, you can specify group policy settings that suppress the reboot until manually enacted, which is a more sensible idea.

To help understand this, let's look at the default rule that exists out of the box. This can be seen in Figure 6-9.

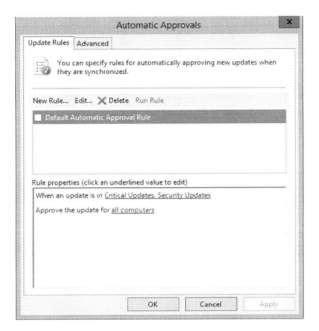

Figure 6-9. *Automatic approval rules*

In this graphic you can see that by default all clients would receive critical updates and security updates. From earlier in the chapter you'll recall these are arguably the most important update types, so this ensures that computers have a certain level of protection from vulnerabilities that could affect them.

Other rules can be established that have the following properties:

- Update classification type (e.g., definition updates)

- Specific product (e.g., Windows Defender)

- Deadline (e.g., within two days of approval)

- Computer Groups (e.g., all computers)

The previous example would relieve a lot of administrative effort, as it would be desirable to have Windows Defender up to date with malware definitions without needing to manually approve this daily.

From time to time, administrators may want to decline an update. For example, it may be desirable to prevent a feature update from installing when it has been determined unnecessary or may cause compatibility problems internally. At any given point, the WSUS admin can decline an update, even if it has been delivered to other computers previously.

Configuring Clients

For a client (and this can be server as well as client operating systems) to connect with and use WSUS, the computer must have some settings configured. These can be configured via either the Registry or Group Policy. You may recall from Figures 6-1, 6-2, and 6-3 that there is not a way to do that through the Control Panel or the Settings app in Windows 10.

If using the Registry, use the following sub key: HKEY_LOCAL_MACHINE\Software\Policies\Microsoft\Windows\WindowsUpdate

The minimum that must be configured are the keys for WUServer and WUStatusServer. These are the pointers to the WSUS server and are either HTTP or HTTPS URLs, such as HTTP://WSUS.Apress.com. Other optional settings will be discussed shortly.

The preferred route, however, is to use Group Policy, either by using a Group Policy Object (GPO) in Active Directory or by using the local Group Policy editor tool on a non-domain-joined computer.

▓ **Note** Domain membership of computers using WSUS is not important, but almost by definition, the fact there is a WSUS server indicates an infrastructure in place that would typically include Active Directory.

In the Group Policy editor, navigate to Computer Configuration ➤ Policies ➤ Administrative Templates ➤ Windows Components ➤ Windows Update.

Figure 6-10 shows the Group Policy settings available. Note that these do not all relate to WSUS usage; most of these can be used even if using Microsoft Update directly.

Setting	State	Comment
Do not display 'Install Updates and Shut Down' option in Sh...	Not configured	No
Do not adjust default option to 'Install Updates and Shut Do...	Not configured	No
Enabling Windows Update Power Management to automati...	Not configured	No
Always automatically restart at the scheduled time	Not configured	No
Configure Automatic Updates	Not configured	No
Specify intranet Microsoft update service location	Not configured	No
Defer Upgrades and Updates	Not configured	No
Automatic Updates detection frequency	Not configured	No
Do not connect to any Windows Update Internet locations	Not configured	No
Allow non-administrators to receive update notifications	Not configured	No
Turn on Software Notifications	Not configured	No
Allow Automatic Updates immediate installation	Not configured	No
Turn on recommended updates via Automatic Updates	Not configured	No
No auto-restart with logged on users for scheduled automat...	Not configured	No
Re-prompt for restart with scheduled installations	Not configured	No
Delay Restart for scheduled installations	Not configured	No
Reschedule Automatic Updates scheduled installations	Not configured	No
Enable client-side targeting	Not configured	No
Allow signed updates from an intranet Microsoft update ser...	Not configured	No

Figure 6-10. *Group Policy settings*

The highlighted setting "Specify intranet Microsoft update service location" is the equivalent setting to the Registry key mentioned earlier. Three other important related settings of note are:

- Defer Upgrades and Updates – This setting, discussed earlier, *will be ignored* if configured if the "Specify intranet . . ." setting is also configured.

- Enable client-side targeting – This can be used to create the computer groups used for update approval and automatic approval rules. Any text string value can be used here, such as Desktop Computers or Laptop Computers, if an admin needs to distinguish different computers for approval reasons.

- Configure Automatic Updates – This is typically set to a value of 4, where the admin wishes to enforce that the client automatically downloads the updates to the computer and schedules an installation of those updates (default is at 3am each day). If the computer is not on at 3am, then whenever the computer is next on after that time is used; for a typical desktop PC this would be first thing in the morning the next day. (This is equivalent to the setting "Install updates automatically (recommended)" from Table 6-3 earlier in the Control Panel settings).

After configuring a client to use WSUS, the computer can either be rebooted or just wait for the settings to kick in on the next sync cycle (the setting for which is the "Automatic Updates detection frequency" option from Group Policy, which has a default value of 22 hours). So, within a day of being configured, you should expect to see the client start to show up in the reporting in the WSUS administration console. We will take a look at this in the next section.

Let's take a look at a summary of the remaining Group Policy settings for completeness. These are shown in Table 6-5 and apply to all Windows client versions unless otherwise indicated.

Table 6-5. *Group Policy Settings*

Setting	Explanation
Do not display "Install Updates and Shut Down" option in Shut Down Windows dialog box.	Toggles whether or not to show to users the option of installing updates upon shutdown, even if there are updates ready to install. Applies to Windows XP SP2, Vista, 7.
Do not adjust default option to "Install Updates and Shut Down" in Shut Down Windows dialog box.	Whether or not "Install Updates and Shut Down" can be used as a default option, else the last shutdown choice selected is shown.
Enabling Windows Update Power Management to automatically wake up the system to install scheduled updates.	Unless on battery power, the PC will wake from sleep/hibernation to install updates at the configured time. Applies to Windows XP SP2, Vista, 7.
Always automatically restart at the scheduled time.	A reset timer showing 15 minutes displays after installing updates instead of showing on the login screen for two days. Applies to Windows 8/RT.
Automatic Updates detection frequency.	Interval used to check for updates. In actual fact, a figure of up to 20 percent of this value is taken off the time set. For example, if 20 hours was configured, then somewhere between 16 and 20 hours is used to randomize different computers for load reasons. Default is 22. Applies to XP and above (except RT).
Do not connect to any Windows Update Internet locations.	Despite a computer being configured to use WSUS, it will still use the Internet location periodically for Microsoft Update or the Store. This prevents those connections. Applies to Windows 8.1 and above.
Allow non-administrator users to receive update notifications.	Older operating systems before Windows 8 did not show standard users update notifications, so they would not see a prompt to install updates if some were pending. This is already configured this way for Windows 8 and above anyway. Applies from Windows XP.

(continued)

159

***Table* 6-5.** (*continued*)

Setting	Explanation
Turn on software notifications.	Gives users using Microsoft Update information on optional applications available. It's disabled by default. Applies to Windows Vista and 7.
Allow Automatic Updates immediate installation.	Should updates that do not reboot the PC or restart services be installed as soon as they are downloaded? Applies from Windows 2000 through 8.1.
Turn on recommended updates via Automatic Updates	Will important as well as recommended updates be downloaded? Default depends on computer's existing setting. Applies from Windows Vista through 8.1.
No auto-restart with logged-on users for scheduled Automatic Updates installations.	If a user is logged on, the PC waits for the user to restart it if required, rather than performing the reboot automatically. Users receive a five-minute warning before reboot if set to "disabled" otherwise. Applies to Windows 2000 and above.
Reprompt for restart for scheduled installations.	Like a snooze button action on an alarm clock. If a user postpones the reboot (if required) after update installation, then how long before displaying the prompt to reboot again? Default is ten minutes. Applies from Windows 2000 through 7.
Delay restart for scheduled installations.	Wait time before a scheduled restart occurs after update installation completes. Applies from Windows 2000 through 7.
Reschedule Automatic Updates scheduled installations.	Wait time after a boot before previously missed scheduled installations proceed. Default is one minute. Applies from Windows 2000 through 7.
Allow signed updates from an intranet Microsoft Update service location.	Whether to accept updates that are signed by third-parties when delivered from WSUS. Applies to XP and above (except RT).

You can tell from the table that some settings either do not apply to the most recent Windows versions or are moot if the computer is configured to use WSUS such that the administrator would decide what type of updates the computer would receive. Be aware that some settings can null others. For example, deferring updates will not have any effect if the computer is set to use a WSUS server and the administrator uses approval rules or manual approval for updates/upgrades anyway.

Troubleshooting and Repairing Windows Update Issues

There are many moving parts when it comes to troubleshooting Windows Update issues on client computers. It is recommended to follow a logical troubleshooting methodology to help get to the bottom of the issue(s).

For example, is the computer connected to the corporate network or Internet, depending on whether WSUS or Microsoft Update is being used? Can the update source be reached; can you ping it?

Let's spend some time looking into some possible causes and look also at some solutions.

Source Configuration

First, it's a good idea to establish what the source of updates is for the computer. You can validate this by using the Registry or Group Policy settings shown previously to determine how the computer is configured. A value for the intranet update service must also be accompanied with a setting for the intranet statistics server. Usually these are the same server. In other words, if these are configured then the computer is using WSUS; if they are not, we can assume it is using Microsoft Update.

Most intranets use HTTP paths for these addresses. Sometimes SSL has been configured, and while principally it is the same service being accessed, the ports being used are different, which may have a bearing on any firewall ports that may be open/closed in between the client and update server. These are pretty standard ports, however, using TCP port 80 or 443 depending on whether HTTP or HTTPS is used, respectively.

Another cause for failure to connect can be that if using HTTPS, the certificate installed on the server needs to be from a certificate authority that the client trusts and can't be expired. All certificates will expire at some point, and it could be that the administrator configured a one- or two-year certificate. All of a sudden it stops working for everyone when it was working fine yesterday. This could be the result of an invalid or expired certificate.

If you are having difficulty determining the Group Policy settings—for instance, you don't have the ability to launch the group policy editor tool—then try using GPresult. exe /V or /Z from a command prompt. GPResult is used to show what settings have been configured in Group Policy and from which policy: local-, domain-, or OU-based policy? In MMC.exe you can also try adding the Resultant Set of Policy snap-in and generating RSoP Data, which will show you the same output. This can help to show if the computer is configured to use the correct WSUS server, for example.

Detection

Don't forget that the default cycle for a client to check in with the server (either WSUS or Microsoft Update) is 22 hours. There can be a natural lag, therefore, from configuring a GPO, having that GPO picked up by a client, starting to use that new setting, and checking in with the new server. Patience can sometimes count for a lot here, especially if it's a new computer being set up on the network for the first time.

There is a way to force the Windows Update component to check for updates–in other words, to avoid waiting another 22 hours for the next cycle. In a command prompt, type `wuauclt.exe /detectnow`. Don't expect to see much in the command prompt to show the success or failure of this! What you are doing is queuing the process that starts detection, which involves the computer going away and having a look at what is has installed and what updates are available on the update server, then computing the differences that need to be downloaded and installed. If an update task is in mid-flow, then the new request gets queued behind it.

■ **Tip**   Patience is key when troubleshooting! Detection cycles and reporting lags are to be expected. It's tricky to appreciate on a modern PC that there should be so much waiting around, but it is recommended to wait a day or two before sweating on an update problem. Reasons include waiting for new Group Policy changes to be detected and applied, waiting for the update cycle to begin, and waiting for reporting in the database to have occurred.

You can check the results of detection activities in Event Viewer, more specifically in Applications and Services Logs ➤ Microsoft ➤ Windows ➤ WindowsUpdateClient ➤ Operational Log. This log can also be used for diagnosing and reporting on a wider set of issues around updates.

In operating systems older than Windows 10, you can also check the log information recorded in `C:\Windows\Windowsupdate.log`. This gives more detailed information that can be used for troubleshooting.

For newer operating systems like Windows 10, there is a PowerShell cmdlet called `Get-WindowsUpdateLog` that takes the content saved in event-tracing format and stored in `C:\Windows\Logs\WindowsUpdate` and converts it into a readable text file on the desktop of the user. This is equivalent to the output that would previously otherwise be found in `C:\Windows\Windowsupdate.log`. You will need to refer to online resources like TechNet to interpret this information, as it does not include header information or code-number lookups.

Metered Connections

When a Windows computer is connected to a WiFi network, it attempts to assess whether the connection is using mobile broadband, such as over a tethered Internet connection using your phone's built-in mobile hotspot functionality. Since Windows 8.1, these types of connections can be classed as 'metered connections,' either automatically via detection by the operating system or manually by the user.

It is by design that Windows updating activities are suspended over metered networks. This would, for example, prevent 3G/4G mobile data plans from being depleted by the volume of network traffic that can occur, especially if a new upgrade build is detected. You can check a computer's metered state in the Settings app, under Network & Internet ➤ WiFi ➤ Advanced Options, as shown in Figure 6-11.

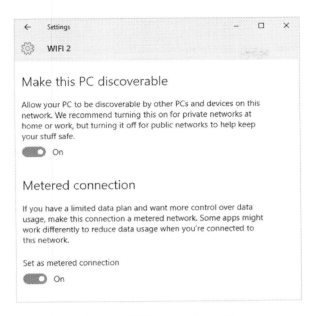

Figure 6-11. *Metered WiFi connection settings*

Services

Looking back at the services that were discussed earlier in this chapter, it is well worth checking to see if they are all correctly running. You should find that both the BITS and Windows Update services are in a running state when your computers are working correctly. If you need to, you can restart them, but often this will not produce a quick turnaround on results due to the intervals mentioned in the previous tip.

Targeting

If the client-side targeting Group Policy setting has been used in conjunction with WSUS, then the computer will belong to a computer group in WSUS. You will recall that update approvals can be targeted at one or more computer groups. These can also be hierarchically configured. For example, you can have a top-level group called Client Computers that contains two subgroups underneath named Laptops and Desktops. This gives you the flexibility of being able to target approved updates to either the Laptops or Desktops group individually, or to all Client Computers at once. Despite the name, it is not assured that just because a computer is a laptop it necessarily is in the correct group, because incorrect targeting of the Group Policy setting could misplace it.

Computer group membership can also be set server-side in the WSUS administration console, whereby an administrator can manually create groups or drag and drop computers between groups. You can also end up with a situation where groups are created manually, but the Group Policy settings may deploy a differently spelled version of the same name. This would result in the computer(s)' not having the appropriate updates approved to them, and they may not pick up some or all updates in the expected way as a result. This is shown in Figure 6-12, where an accidental typo has resulted in the wrong name for the Desktops group.

It's worth pointing out the catch-all group called Unassigned Computers, which is where computers end up that did not have client-side or server-side targeting configured. Again, the state of approvals of updates for this set of computers could be at odds with other correctly configured computers. It's recommended that you check to see if there are any computers in that group and either manually move them or modify Group Policy settings to align them to the intended group, or to ensure that that group is used for approving updates. For instance, you could create an automatic approval rule that approved all update classifications for all products downloaded to that group. That way they would always get updates, but not perhaps in the staggered way that other correctly configured computers would.

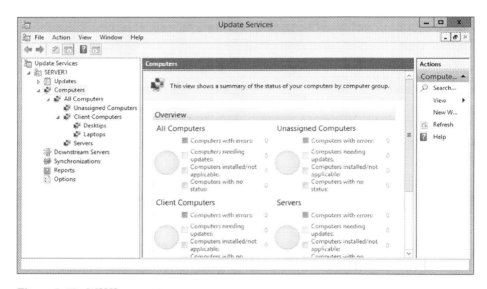

Figure 6-12. *WSUS computer groups*

Reporting

You can also see the state of compliance in the summary pie charts in Figure 6-12, which are displayed for each of the computer groups in the middle pane. Further drill-down is required for individual computers, which can be achieved using the Reports node in the same tool.

In the WSUS console, there are three different types of reports that an administrator can access, as follows:

- Update Reports – shows the status of updates, such as approval state

- Computer Reports – computer orientated view to show which updates does a given computer have, or group of computers

- Synchronization Reports – state of last syncs with Microsoft Update

These reports give very granular insight into the state of a given update or a given computer. For instance, you would be able to tell which updates had installed correctly, failed to install, or are required but not yet installed for a given computer. You could also examine a specific update to see which computers it was installed onto or had failed to install onto. Using reports as a troubleshooting tool can be very effective courtesy of the depth of information sent to the database by the clients during the update checks.

Other Network-Related Issues

As mentioned earlier, there are many moving parts here that could cause issues with updating computers. Assuming that Control Panel, the Settings app, or Group Policy are correctly configured, there are other checks you can perform, such as the ones below:

TCP/IP Configuration – Does the client have an appropriate IP address, subnet mask, DNS server, and default gateway for the network?

Name Resolution – Does the client successfully resolve the endpoint (WSUS or Microsoft Update) name?

Firewall Access – Can the client reach the desired server endpoint using HTTP(S)? In actual fact, there are quite a few names that are documented on Microsoft's website that may be used by Microsoft Update or WSUS synchronizations, such as `http://windowsupdate.microsoft.com` and `http://*.windowsupdate.com`. For access to WSUS, computers typically use ports 80/443, but they can also use 8530 and 8531, so it's worth checking what's used and what ports are open on the server or any other devices that lie between the client and the server.

Summary

Keeping Windows up to date is highly recommended so as to maintain good protection from malicious attacks, malware, and bugs. To reduce the likelihood of attack through a known vulnerability, Microsoft will adopt a more forceful approach to updates in the future. For the consumer users of Windows 10, all updates and upgrades will automatically be applied to devices. You have seen how enterprises will be able to manage updates using Group Policy and WSUS.

Devices that are typically located outside of your corporate network pose additional challenges in relation to how you can manage and maintain them. In the final chapter, you will learn how you can manage devices using Microsoft Intune, which is especially useful for the management of devices used outside of the corporate environment.

CHAPTER 7

■ ■ ■

Managing Windows Updates with Intune

Today's modern workplace is very different than that which existed ten to fifteen years ago. At that time, users would typically use a desktop PC or laptop, but would mostly work from the same office each day. Occasionally, they would visit a customer, but for the most part administrators had pretty good fingertip control over the computers they managed. Typically, client computers would be domain joined, and administrators enjoyed a high level of management control using services like Active Directory and Group Policy.

Today is different. Laptops and tablets outsell desktop computers, and many users work for extended periods away from their main desk or, in some cases, never go into the office at all, always working remotely. The concepts of Bring Your Own Device (BYOD) and Choose Your Own Device (CYOD) are phenomena that administrators have had to wrangle with in recent years.

This had led to a need for a more open approach to PC and device management that extends beyond an organization's traditional four walls. Modern workers demand greater freedom of movement and flexibility, but at the same time administrators are under pressure to deliver device security and ensure that corporate data can be safely accessed by trusted users.

Cloud-based services that address this need for modern device management have been quickly evolving over the last two to three years. Microsoft has been at the cutting edge of this wave of change and has been offering Microsoft Intune as a service that allows administrators to manage a diverse range of modern devices from the cloud.

Overview of Microsoft Intune

Microsoft Intune is a cloud-based service that organizations can subscribe to. It encompasses services that you may expect to find in a modern enterprise network, but that are accessed instead from the cloud. These services act and work very much like their on-premise equivalent services. The main difference is that the administrator does not own and manage the platform directly. Instead, the organization is a tenant within a much larger system.

© Chris Rhodes and Andrew Bettany 2016
C. Rhodes and A. Bettany, *Windows Installation and Update Troubleshooting*,
DOI 10.1007/978-1-4842-1827-3_7

This becomes attractive to systems administrators for various reasons. First, the organization is free of network infrastructure costs. No WSUS server, Active Directory domain controllers, DNS servers, or any kind of server are required. Organizations just need clients, a subscription, and an Internet connection. That's it.

Clients need not be domain joined. In fact, they do not have to be connected to a corporate network of any kind. The clients simply need Internet connectivity. This enables the administrator to support users who work in the field from a customer site, or even home-based workers, with the same level of control.

Like many cloud services, Microsoft Intune is a moving target in terms of functionality, as Microsoft will, from time to time, roll out new features. As they manage the backend service, there is no interaction required by administrators to receive the new updates to the service.

The main features that are part of Microsoft Intune are:

- Mobile Device Management (MDM)

- Mobile Application Management

- Windows Firewall Management

- Endpoint Protection

- Selective wipe capability of applications and data from devices

- Hardware and software inventories and reports

Much of Microsoft Intunes' functionality mirrors that of System Center 2012 Configuration Manager. System Center 2012 Configuration Manager (SCCM) is one of the components of System Center that can be used to manage clients and servers on a corporate network. For many administrators of small- and medium-sized organizations, the cost, skills, and management required to run SCCM make it not viable.

Intune allows even very small organizations to leverage SCCM-style features at a fraction of the cost within minutes of provisioning the service. For example, an administrator can drill down to examine how many of the managed devices have a particular application installed or to see which updates are installed on each device.

Integrating Intune

It is worth noting that Intune can also be a part of an Office 365 subscription. For those organizations that have a commercial subscription to Office 365, such as an E3 subscription, the MDM capabilities of Office 365–such as policy controls and device wipe–are actually components of Intune.

Crucially for customers who use Microsoft Enterprise Mobility Suite (EMS), Intune is a core component of the identity and management toolset. Intune provides the MDM and application management components. It can also be tightly integrated with installations of Microsoft System Center 2012 Configuration Manager for the unified management of computers and devices based on the premises and cloud-based devices, giving administrators single-pane management of all the devices that they manage whether they exist in the corporate network or not.

Creating a Microsoft Intune Subscription

Before creating a Microsoft Intune subscription, it is worth reviewing how the organization will be using the service and which clients they intend to enroll and manage.

In terms of how the organization will use the service, careful planning must occur when connecting Intune with Exchange Server or System Center 2012 Configuration Manager. This, however, is beyond the scope of this chapter.

Supported Clients

Microsoft Intune supports a wide range of clients that run Windows, iOS, and Android. However, it is important to distinguish here the different ways that clients can interact with Intune. Our goal for this chapter is to learn how to manage Windows updates using Intune. As such, the clients must obviously be running not only Windows, but also the Intune client software that is downloaded from the management portal. This is referred to as *Managing Computers* in the Intune portal. We will explore this in more detail shortly. This software gives us full-fidelity management of our clients, including inventory and policies, as well as Endpoint protection and Windows updates.

The other way that clients can enroll in Intune is by using the client's built-in MDM capabilities. Modern mobile operating systems, as found on iOS-, Android-, and Windows-based phones, tablets, and other devices, come with MDM client software. This links to a management authority that controls policies, such as security and encryption settings, on the device. This is referred to as M*anaging Mobile Devices* in the management portal, as shown in Figure 7-1.

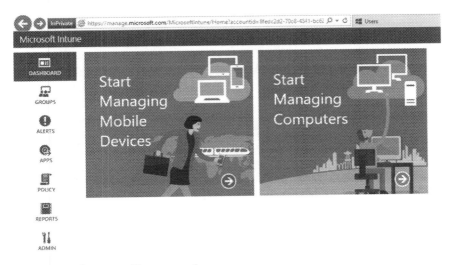

Figure 7-1. *Computer Management*

For the purposes of the rest of this chapter, we will focus on clients that enrolled by installing the client software, and that can therefore take advantage of the ability to control Windows updates (Managing Computers). Table 7-1 shows the supported list of clients that can be managed in this way.

Table 7-1. *Supported Microsoft Intune–Managed Computers*

Operating System	Editions (x86 & x64)
Windows Vista	Business, Enterprise, Ultimate
Windows 7	Professional, Enterprise, Ultimate
Windows 8	Pro, Enterprise
Windows 8.1	Pro, Enterprise
Windows 10	Pro, Enterprise

Aside from the operating system version and editions, and the need for Internet connectivity, the only other requirement is that the client installation software be installed by a user that is a member of the local administrators group.

▓ **Note** Due to the technical similarities with System Center 2012 Configuration Manager, Intune-managed devices cannot be running the client agent software for SCCM 2012 or earlier versions. These *must* be uninstalled before enrolling a device in Intune.

Subscriptions

The best way to learn Microsoft Intune is to create a subscription. You can create a trial subscription by following these steps:

1. Create a tenant subscription in Intune. The easiest way to do that is by connecting to **http://www.microsoft.com/ intune**. From there, a free trial can be set up that can later be converted into a paid subscription. The way that Intune is licensed is per user, not per device, so it would be possible for a user to own several devices that were all connected to Intune and only pay for that one user. The approximate cost is $6 USD per user (although this can change and will be converted to local currencies; for example, in the United Kingdom this works out to be £3.70, factoring in currency and taxes).

2. Create the subscription based on using Intune as a standalone service (as opposed to integrating with System Center 2012 Configuration Manager) as it is more straightforward. First, fill in the form as shown in Figure 7-2. It will default to one license, but you can add more licenses on the next page and then go through the checkout process. More licenses can be added later in the admin area in Intune. For now, let's assume you want to trial Intune as you are learning more about it, so use the Try Now button on-screen instead of purchasing the subscription at this time. This will give you 100 user licenses to play with for 30 days.

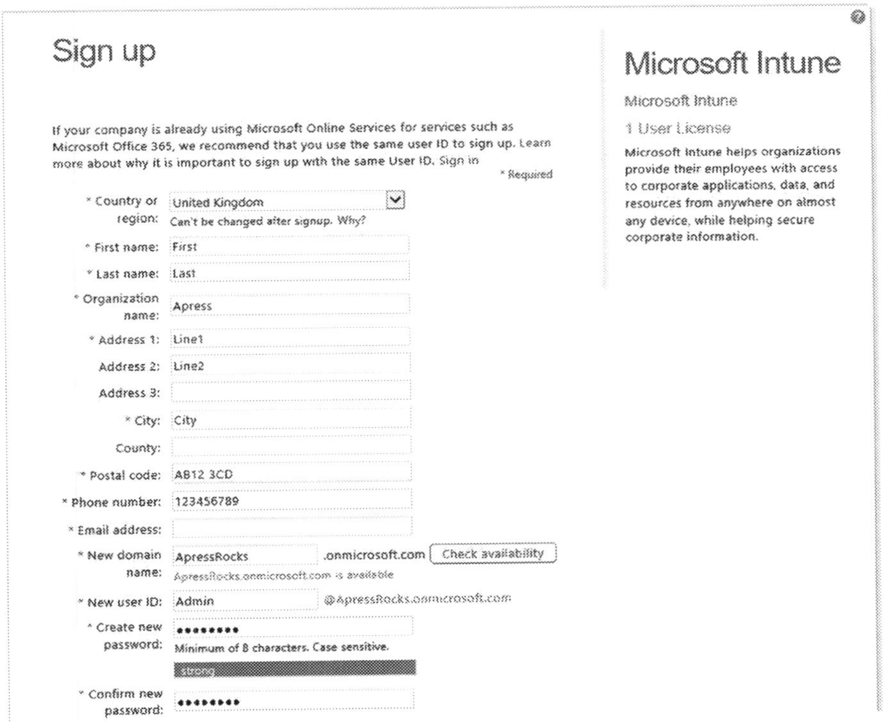

Figure 7-2. Signing up for an Intune subscription

▒ **Note** You will observe in Figure 7-2 that a custom domain name is created as part of the sign-up process in the format of `customer.onmicrosoft.com`. This is the same as the process of creating an Office 365 subscription, and in fact the two share the same backend authentication service, Azure Active Directory. You can also add public domain names that you own into Intune to make user identities easier for users to work with.

3. Once signed up, either with a trial or a paid account, the next step is to add users. This is required so that your end users can then enroll devices into Intune. You are directed to the Account Portal, where there are two choices: adding new users into Intune or using user accounts that already exist, such as in your company's Active Directory, and then using single sign-on. Both options are shown in Figure 7-3. To keep things simple, we will skip Active Directory integration and synchronization to Intune, as we want to focus on updates.

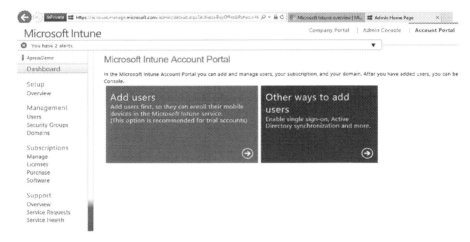

Figure 7-3. *Adding users in Intune*

When creating new users, the domain name that was established in the sign-up is used as the naming suffix. Using Figure 7-2 as an example, a new user could be `User1@ApressRocks.onmicrosoft.com`. The administrator is given the optional choice as to whether to give each new user administrative permissions or just have them as a standard Intune user, as shown in Figure 7-4.

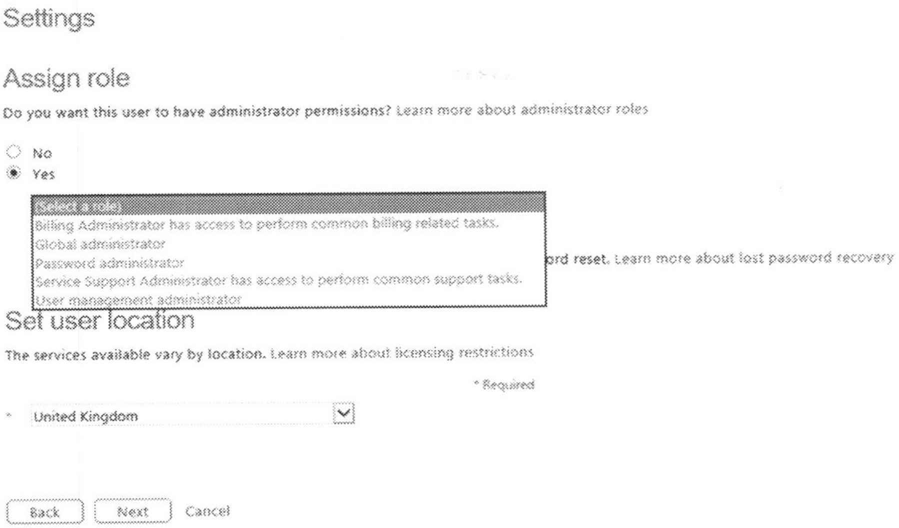

Settings

Assign role

Do you want this user to have administrator permissions? Learn more about administrator roles

○ No
⦿ Yes

> Select a role)
> Billing Administrator has access to perform common billing related tasks.
> Global administrator
> Password administrator   ord reset. Learn more about lost password recovery
> Service Support Administrator has access to perform common support tasks.
> User management administrator

Set user location

The services available vary by location. Learn more about licensing restrictions

* Required

＊ United Kingdom ⌄

[Back] [Next] Cancel

Figure 7-4. *Assigning user roles*

Enrolling Clients

Once user accounts are added, you must navigate to the Admin Console and then to the dashboard to begin managing your devices, as you saw in in Figure 7-1. Remember that Intune can be used not only as an MDM solution for mobile devices, such as tablets and phones, but also as a solution for managing Windows-based PCs by installing the client software.

The client software needs to be installed onto the target computers so that Windows updates can be managed. Exactly how the client software gets onto the PCs is not so important, as long as it does. Here are the main ways that the client software can be deployed:

- Install as part of an operating system image (it is effectively preinstalled when Windows is deployed)

- Deployed through Active Directory Group Policy (the computer needs to be domain joined)

- Local user installs the software (local administrator access required on the computer)

- Users access the Intune Company Portal and self-enroll (local administrative access required. Internet Explorer required also)

Once a computer is enrolled, the computer is linked to the user account that was used to install the client software. It is worth noting that Microsoft Intune Endpoint Protection is also installed by default. Endpoint Protection is the enterprise protection software that helps to protect against viruses and malicious software.

■ **Note** The amount of bandwidth required to run an Intune-enrolled device varies, but is approximately 10 MB per day. This allows for the device to check in with Intune cloud services to report hardware and software inventory, Windows updates, and policy checks and to download Endpoint Protection updates.

To install the client software, you must first download it from the Admin node of the Intune portal. The download is a single zip file that contains an installation file named `Microsoft_Intune_Setup.exe`, which is generic to all Intune tenants, and a specific certificate named `MicrosoftIntune.accountcert`, which identifies the client to that particular organization's tenant account in Intune.

Once installed, the client software installs agents that will report into Intune over the Internet on the status, such as the hardware and software inventory and which Windows updates clients have deployed. Once the client is installed and the computer has checked in to Intune for the first time, the computer should be visible in the Admin Console, as shown in Figure 7-5.

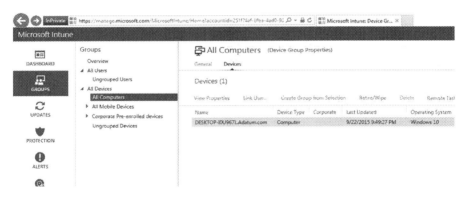

Figure 7-5. *Verifiying succesful client installation*

Configuring Microsoft Intune Updates

Once you have your subscription created and your clients connected to Intune, it's time to turn your attention to how you will manage updates using Intune. In Chapter 6, we covered how WSUS works for devices that connect to the corporate network for updates. In simple terms, Intune is really a WSUS service in the cloud. Most of the principles and knowledge learned about WSUS management apply here too.

In fact, the similarities are such that it is easier to explain how they are different. In Chapter 6, we discussed how WSUS servers can be configured either to store updates locally or to never store updates and have the clients obtain the files from the Internet instead. In the case of Intune, there is no choice, as updates always come from the Internet.

Also, Intune does not support driver updates at this time, so drivers would need to be managed separately by Windows or as part of an image (see Chapter 4).

▦ **Note**   WSUS can bring greater efficiency to the network, as updates only need to be downloaded once to the server, and then all clients can obtain the update from the intranet. This caching not only saves bandwidth, but also means that clients that are not up to date can become compliant without touching the Internet and therefore without being at risk from an exploit that a security update may otherwise protect against. This is a potential disadvantage with Intune that needs to be considered.

Figure 7-6 shows an overview of the Intune Updates node in the console. From here the administrator can access reports, add new updates to manage, and configure settings such as automatic approval rules, which we will discuss in more detail in the following pages.

Figure 7-6. *Intune Updates node*

Let's start by looking at the update classifications as seen in Figure 7-6. These classifications mirror the options a WSUS administrator would see, with the exception of drivers, which has already been pointed out. Unlike WSUS, the updates available to the tenant administrator of Intune do not need to be synced with Microsoft Update (the main originating source of updates).

By default, an administrator will see an overwhelming amount of back-catalog updates here dating back many years, all of which are *not* approved for install. It may look daunting, but in fact you are not expected to approve each and every update—it would be too time consuming (although if you really wanted to, you could!).

Third-Party Updates

One of the great features of Intune is the ability to add third-party updates for deployment. Now, bear in mind that Intune can also deliver applications to clients anyway–this is not the same thing. Third-party updates are updates that can be deployed in the same way as Microsoft-supplied updates, but are uploaded by the administrator and can be from any vendor. These updates must install silently–that is to say, without user interaction–but can take the form of any of the following file types:

- EXE - traditional executable

- MSI - Windows Installer application

- MSP - Windows Installer patch

Once you have the update in one of the preceding formats, in the Intune Update node, click the Add Updates button to have it download a small uploader application that walks you through the process. You must supply some information, such as publisher and description, and you can also configure requirements, such as an operating architecture (x86/x64) and OS version (e.g., Windows 8.1). Detection rules in Intune are used to ensure that all the computer groups that an update is approved for, would install it once. You can also create a custom rule that looks for a prerequisite, such as the presence of a file or registry key, to help determine whether the update is required for a computer or not. You also need to point it to the dependency software that this depends on having be installed to update. At this point the update is ready to approve, but like all the other updates it is not approved by default.

Approving Updates

As we have learned, the Microsoft and third-party updates will not be installed onto any computers until they are approved by an administrator. In the case of third-party ones, this is not too time consuming, as you are unlikely to have that many, but certainly for the thousands of Windows updates on offer approving every one is not viable.

This sets the stage for *automatic approval rules*. Before we embark on creating these, however, we need to understand the concept of computer groups. As in WSUS, computer groups allow the administrator to segment different sets of computers in any way they want–for example, to differentiate intranet computers and home workers' computers–so that different updates can be applied to each group. There are some default groups, as shown in Figure 7-7.

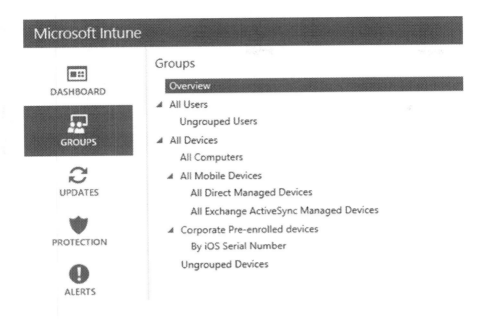

Figure 7-7. *Default groups*

New computers that get enrolled into Intune end up in the All Computers group, but you can create your own custom groups and move computers between them. Alternatively, if you are happy that all computers you manage should be treated the same and have the same updates, it is fine to leave it at that and deploy updates to All Computers.

Back in the Updates node, if you click on Configure Updates, you are taken to Admin ➤ Administration ➤ Updates to set up categories, classifications, and automatic approval rules, as shown in Figure 7-8.

Figure 7-8. *Configuring Updates settings*

One of areas that is worth exploring is the Product Category area, where you can select/deselect products and their respective versions. For example, you can select Windows and then select the versions, such as 7, 8.1 and 10. All Windows versions are selected by default, as Intune is for Windows machines anyway. You must check this from time to time as new versions of software are released to ensure you are covering the products used on your managed computers.

You can see from Figure 7-8 that you can also select Update Classifications, such as Security Updates, Definition Updates, and Critical Updates, to name a few. This list rarely changes, so don't worry too much about this after configuring it for the first time.

The most important section on this page is the Automatic Approval Rules area. This is where you will configure rules that approve updates based on the criteria that you specify. For example, you could create a rule that affects Windows, Skype, and Office versions from the product category, and allows critical as well as security updates, and finally deploys this to the All Computers group. You would repeat as needed until you have fulfilled the business logic for each computer group you defined.

░ **Tip**   It is a good idea to run the new rule after you create it to push along the process of getting the first batch of updates out to the computers. This will then apply the rule logic to the updates collection.

Bear in mind, however, that there are sometimes updates that require manual approval. This is sometimes because there might be a functionality change or an end-user licence agreement that requires administrative approval, despite the rules you have set up. Sometimes this is also because the update cannot be uninstalled once installed. These updates that require manual approval are called out for you, as you saw in Figure 7-6 earlier.

It is worth mentioning that updates can also be declined. For example, you may not want the functionality change an update could bring, or you may want to suppress an update until an application can be tested first.

Reports

As in WSUS, one of the most valuable facets of using Intune for update management is the ability to view drill-down reporting. You can create an update report (among other reports, such as detected software for inventory of applications on computers) for specific groups or for all groups, and also specify the types of updates you want to include. Figure 7-9 shows an example report that displays the state of updates, with a focus on a specific update, showing which computers need the update, which have it already, and which have failed to install it.

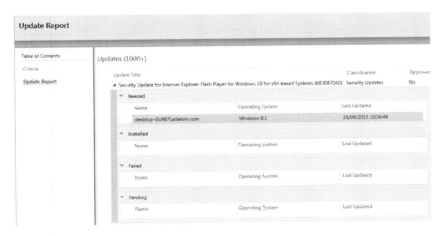

Figure 7-9. *Sample update report*

This kind of cloud-based reporting is invaluable and really underlines the value in using Intune for checking the compliance of remote computers.

Agent Settings

In the same way that automatic approval rules can be created to affect the way different computers apply updates, the Intune client agent can also be configured in a *configuration policy*. You will find these configuration policies in Policy ➤ Add ➤ Computer Management ➤ Microsoft Intune Agent Settings.

There are numerous areas such Endpoint Protection settings that can be configured in the Intune Agent configuration policy, but Figure 7-10 shows the section related to updates.

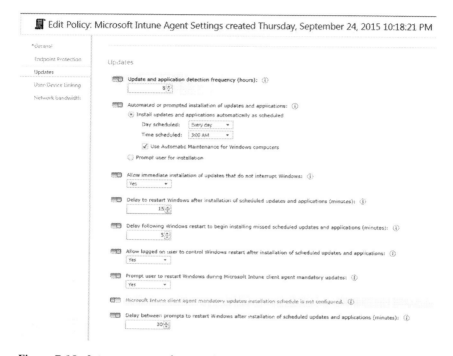

Figure 7-10. *Intune agent updates settings*

A summary of some of the settings is shown in Table 7-2, which is useful for the upcoming section on troubleshooting.

Table 7-2. *Default Update Policy Settings*

Setting	Value
Update and application detection frequency	8 hours
Install updates and applications automatically as scheduled	Every day, 03:00am
Delay following Windows restart to begin installing missed scheduled updates and applications	5 minutes

Troubleshooting Microsoft Intune Updates

Troubleshooting Intune clients can be tricky from the outset, as they can simply be Internet-connected Windows computers that you do not have direct contact with in the same way you would traditionally manage desktop PCs within a corporate environment.

You must approach troubleshooting Intune-managed updates systematically to ensure success.

First, start by verifying that the client is listed as a managed client in the Intune Admin Console. You can do this by looking in Groups ➤ All Devices ➤ All Computers. You can see an enrolled client in Figure 7-11, along with its computer name, when it last updated, and other useful information.

Figure 7-11. *Enrolled devices list*

If the computer is not even listed here, then there is an issue with the client not communicating with the Intune services, or the client software was not successfully installed. Communications failures are hard to diagnose remotely, as you may not have physical access to the computer. First, try to identify whether the issue is a generic Internet access problem or whether it is just the Intune servers that cannot be accessed. Do not overlook proxy servers that may exist between the computer and the Internet as well.

▓ **Tip**   A simple way of testing whether a client can access Intune services over the Internet is to try and access `https://manage.microsoft.com` from a web browser on the computer. If this cannot be reached, then there is either a DNS or Internet access issue or the service is down. To check the status of Intune services, visit `https://status.manage.microsoft.com/StatusPage/ServiceDashboard`

Bookmarking the Service Dashboard URL can be a fast way of verifying whether a connectivity issue is likely to affect lots of devices, or indeed if the problem exists at the user's device rather than in the cloud, or any other transient Internet issue. Figure 7-12 shows the current status of service in each Intune datacenter location.

Microsoft Intune

Current Status
The current service status is shown in the following table. Move the pointer over the status icon to view more information when available.

Status	Service Instance	Details	
◎	Asia 01	The service instance is running normally.	▨
◎	Asia 02	The service instance is running normally.	▨
◎	Asia 03	The service instance is running normally.	▨
◎	Asia 05	The service instance is running normally.	▨
◎	Europe 01	The service instance is running normally.	▨
◎	Europe 02	The service instance is running normally.	▨
◎	Europe 03	The service instance is running normally.	▨
◎	Europe 05	The service instance is running normally.	▨
◎	North America 01	The service instance is running normally.	▨
◎	North America 02	The service instance is running normally.	▨
◎	North America 04	The service instance is running normally.	▨
◎	North America 05	The service instance is running normally.	▨

Figure 7-12. *Intune service status*

Check also that the client software installed successfully. There are numerous error codes that can be reported in the Alerts area of the Admin Console if a client has an issue, but can still connect to Intune. It can be worth attempting to reinstall the client software. This is not as straightforward as finding the application in Programs and Features in the Control Panel and removing it, as it is not visible there. The device needs to be "retired" from the Intune Admin Console, which creates a task to uninstall it. It can then be reinstalled in the same way a client is provisioned for the first time, as was discussed earlier in this chapter.

Checking services is a really good way of determining that the problem does not exist on the client computer. The main Intune-related service is called the Microsoft Online Management Client Service. This should be running, and it communicates with Intune for most of the client-server interactions. The other dependency service to check is Windows Update. This service is the same service that was mentioned in Chapter 6, but it will have been modified to point to Intune for management while working in the same way.

One possible reason why a domain-joined client may not be reporting in an update status to Intune is a conflict with Group Policy Object (GPO) settings. Consider this example: you have deployed WSUS to manage desktop computers and created a GPO that configures those machines to use the WSUS server as the point for updates. You have some domain-joined clients that are supposed to be managed by Intune, but actually pick up the WSUS server GPO settings, in which case GPO will win over the Intune settings and the client will use WSUS only. Use GPResult.exe /Z or the Resultant Set of Policy MMC snap-in to diagnose whether this is the case. You should exclude computers in this type of scenario from being affected by such a policy.

Patience!

One thing that IT professionals are known for is being impatient. We expect to click a button and "Hey, Presto!" it's done. Well, sort of. With Intune, there are several intervals during which an administrator should be patient and wait for before throwing the towel in. These are summarized next, with default values taken from Table 7-2:

- Time from installation of client software to it being reported in the Admin Console: 30 minutes. (Typically, it's less than this, but to manage expectations, Microsoft recommends waiting at least this length of time before troubleshooting.)

- Time for approved updates to show as needed on a computer (up to eight hours for detection frequency)

- Time for approved updates to download to client (depends on type of update and whether there is a deadline for the update)

- Time for downloaded update to install (03:00 every day, or when the computer is next booted if missed)

- Time for installed updates to be reported back to Intune. (This works in the detection cycle, like checking for updates, so it can show a false picture in the short term where computers may be up to date but Intune is not aware of that yet).

In other words, do not expect an even, universal view of the managed PCs in the short term. Things will work themselves out, and computers that have an update approved to them should get the update downloaded, installed, and reported back to Intune in due course. In the short term, however, expect that some computers will not be switched on, will not be connected to the Internet, or will be waiting for scheduled check-ins before acting on instructions. Don't forget, these are configurable as well!

Summary

In this chapter, we have seen how Microsoft Intune can be used to manage updates for clients even if they are remote from the corporate network. The Intune administrator has a few configuration tasks that are unique to that service, such as initially adding the client agent software to devices so that they can be managed. Once under the control of Intune, many aspects of update management are very similar to what you saw in Chapter 6. Certainly as a skillset, an administrator with experience of WSUS will not have a steep learning curve, though they will need to adapt what they know about on premise–based update management to how it works in the cloud.

We hope that you have enjoyed reading this book and that it has given you much greater insight into installing and updating Windows, whether that is on a per computer basis or at scale on a larger network using services such as WDS and WSUS.

You should now feel more confident that you know how Windows can be installed or upgraded and kept updated, and how administrators can deploy it at scale over a network using lite-touch or zero-touch methods via MDT and SCCM. Importantly, you also know how to keep Windows plugged into the update and upgrade cadence that Microsoft introduced with Windows 10, so that your devices will remain protected and up to date and you can control and have ownership of the process, whether you are using SCCM, WSUS, or Intune to manage the clients.

Now, it's your turn to take what you have read about and start using the tools that we have described throughout the book!

Andrew & Chris

Index

© Chris Rhodes and Andrew Bettany 2016
C. Rhodes and A. Bettany, *Windows Installation and Update Troubleshooting*,
DOI 10.1007/978-1-4842-1827-3

Get the eBook for only $5!

Why limit yourself?

Now you can take the weightless companion with you wherever you go and access your content on your PC, phone, tablet, or reader.

Since you've purchased this print book, we're happy to offer you the eBook in all 3 formats for just $5.

Convenient and fully searchable, the PDF version enables you to easily find and copy code—or perform examples by quickly toggling between instructions and applications. The MOBI format is ideal for your Kindle, while the ePUB can be utilized on a variety of mobile devices.

To learn more, go to www.apress.com/companion or contact support@apress.com.

Printed in the United States
By Bookmasters